THE LIBRARY OF HOLOCAUST TESTIMONIES

No Strength to Forget

The Library of Holocaust Testimonies

Editors: Antony Polonsky, Sir Martin Gilbert CBE, Aubrey Newman,
Raphael F. Scharf, Ben Helfgott MBE

Under the auspices of the Yad Vashem Committee of the Board of
Deputies of British Jews and the Centre for Holocaust Studies,
University of Leicester

No Strength to Forget

Survival in the Ukraine, 1941–1944

LAIZER BLITT

VALLENTINE MITCHELL
LONDON • PORTLAND, OR

First published in 2007 in Great Britain by
VALLENTINE MITCHELL
Suite 314, Premier House
Edgware, Middlesex HA8 7BJ

and in the United States of America by
VALLENTINE MITCHELL
c/o ISBS, 920 NE 58th Avenue, Suite 300
Portland, Oregon 97213-3786

www.vmbooks.com

British Library Cataloguing in Publication Data

A catalogue record has been applied for

ISBN 978 0 85303 696 8
ISSN 1363 3759

Library of Congress Cataloging-in-Publication Data

A catalogue record has been applied for

Printed in Great Britain by Biddles Ltd, King's Lynn, Norfolk

Contents

Dedicated to the memory of my parents
Mordechai Aryeh (Leib) Blitt
Adele Blitt née Ruttenberg

The Library of Holocaust Testimonies

Ten years have passed since Frank Cass launched his Library of Holocaust Testimonies. It was greatly to his credit that this was done, and even more remarkable that it has continued and flourished. The memoirs of each survivor throw new light and cast new perspectives on the fate of the Jews of Europe during the Holocaust. No voice is too small or humble to be heard, no story so familiar that it fails to tell the reader something new, something hitherto unnoticed, something previously unknown.

Each new memoir adds to our knowledge not only of the Holocaust, but also of many aspects of the human condition that are universal and timeless: the power of evil and the courage of the oppressed; the cruelty of the bystanders and the heroism of those who sought to help, despite the risks; the part played by family and community; the question of who knew what and when; the responsibility of the wider world for the destructive behaviour of tyrants and their henchmen.

Fifty memoirs are already in print in the Library of Holocaust Testimonies, and several more are being published each year. In this way anyone interested in the Holocaust will be able to draw upon a rich seam of eyewitness accounts. They can also use another Vallentine Mitchell publication, the multi-volume *Holocaust Memoir Digest*, edited by Esther Goldberg, to explore the contents of survivor memoirs in a way that makes them particularly accessible to teachers and students alike.

Sir Martin Gilbert
London, April 2005

1 *This is What I Remember*

It is not my intention to write my biography or to add another document to those dealing with the atrocities of the Holocaust, but to expose only a segment of my life, which I have suppressed for the past forty-five years. I discovered that as I began to commit these events to paper, they were replaced with a greater capacity to absorb life. There are a number of reasons for embarking on this undertaking. To begin with, I wanted my children to have some knowledge of what I experienced during the Holocaust. Secondly, I felt that with the passing of the years, there are fewer survivors left to tell their stories. Above all I realized that I have 'NO STRENGTH TO FORGET'.

From time to time I force myself to read or watch material dealing with the Holocaust. It is always a great effort for me to do so because it brings back, too vividly, my own experiences, which I have tried to forget. In spite of the fact that the material about the Holocaust, with which I come into contact, is genuine, I still feel it represents a futile attempt to explain an event that is beyond human comprehension. It is even more alarming to realize that genocide – the horror of legalized murder – was perpetrated by a supposedly enlightened 'super race', in the name of a new world order – a new ideology.

Some authors writing about the Holocaust, like Elie Wiesel, and other famous personalities, reveal their own experiences as proof and cry out in rage against the world for allowing this to happen. I also am writing about my experiences as child during the Holocaust. My outrage is not against the world, however, but against a group of evil men possessed by an unlimited hatred of mankind. These evil men, who originated from a civilized Western country like Germany, converted people's lives into hell on earth. They converted the world into a bloodbath in which almost fifty million people lost their lives. Six million of the casualties were Jews. It is true that these evil men had an unusually great number of helpers in their demonic goal of world domination. I maintain that although it is possible to describe the Holocaust in detail, with authority and accuracy, the phenomenon itself is impossible to explain or to understand. It is beyond any comprehension: how one human being can reduce another to the level of a rodent. Essentially, I could begin this chapter of my life by saying: 'One day, when I was about 6 years old, I discovered that all Jewish children, like me, had been reduced to the status of rodents. They and their parents, therefore, were to be eliminated from the face of the earth by all possible means, and in the most efficient manner.'

The most revolting efforts to explain the rationale behind the Holocaust come from the mouths of some ultra-orthodox rabbis. Some of them maintain that this was the design of God and that the Nazis were His messengers. Their argument states that the Holocaust is similar to an operation in which a patient is cut up in order to save his life. Only the surgeon knows what he is doing, as only God knows the purpose behind the Holocaust. A more blasphemous uttering I cannot possibly imagine, and I pity the people who believe in such a vengeful and merciless God in heaven. Only Satan in hell could have devised such an evil plan and chosen such black-hearted messengers to execute it.

WELCOME TO KORTILESS

My official documents claim that I was born in the city of Ratno, Poland, in the year 1935. In fact I was born in the *dorf* (village) of Kortiless, Ukraine, which at the time of my birth was occupied by Poland. I make this clarification not because of nationalistic sentiment but because, as I discovered in later years, not all Jews are alike. There seem to be some differences between Polish and Ukrainian Jews. There were differences between the *shtetl* (small city) Jew and the village Jew. What I have discovered, essentially, is that Jewish people throughout the diaspora had the uncanny ability to absorb the characteristics, culture and appearance of their hosts, while at the same time remaining devoted to the cause of perpetuating the Jewish people. They are not 'fossils of history' as Toynbee would want us to believe but an integral part of history, no matter where they lived.

To describe at this point, with any amount of accuracy, the physical layout of Kortiless is an almost impossible task. There are two pictures of Kortiless, however, that are still imprinted on my mind. The first one is that it was about three kilometers long, running from north to south. I know that was the direction, because of a childish observation. We lived in the first Jewish house at the northern entrance to the village, and as I faced towards the other end, I would sometimes see a Ukrainian funeral procession and hear singing. It was a very impressive sight, with many colourful icons and banners, and the priest and his helpers wearing highly-embroidered garments. As the procession neared my house it would turn towards my right, in the direction of the cemetery located on a hill, a couple of hundred meters from where I stood. The sun always set right over the cemetery and I came to the conclusion that the sun went to sleep in the *goyishe* (gentile) cemetery. This fact disturbed me greatly, as I felt it was unfair of the sun to show such partiality.

There was a dirt road that crossed right through the middle of the town. On both sides of the road there were ditches, and little bridges at many points providing access to the houses. At the end of the road was a big circle, dominated by the church, which was the largest structure in the village. On the periphery of that circle was the home of my paternal grandparents and my Uncle Shmuel (Shmilke). Further north, towards the centre of the village, stood the synagogue, and not far from it lived my maternal grandparents and my uncles, Ben Zion (Bentse) and Yerachmiel. They owned one of the most beautiful homes in the village. It contained many rooms – even a separate kitchen – wooden floors, brass handles on the doors, a red shingled roof and a front porch. Attached to the house was a kind of store which contained various goods, including sweets. Behind the store was another room that housed a centrifugal pump, which for a fee separated the cream from the milk for farmers. My grandfather's affluence stemmed from the fact that he had gone to America for a number of years and established a successful soft-drink bottling business. He sold the business and returned to Kortiless because America was not an easy place to maintain a 'good Jewish life'. Incidentally, my paternal grandfather left America for the same reason, although he did not leave behind a successful business, having seen the American way of life only from the confines of a sweatshop.

Across the street from my grandfather, several houses to the north, lived the shochet (ritual slaughterer), who also served the additional functions of rabbi and rebbe (teacher) in the cheder, which was held in his home. About a hundred meters west of the shochet's house was the *mikveh* (ritual bath). The tailor's house was a little way south from ours, on the right-hand side of the road. The tailor had a son who was my age, and my friend. One day we had some difference of opinion that developed into a scrap. He managed to get the better of me but he decided to leave 'the field of battle' while he was still a victor, and took off for his home as fast as his feet would carry him. I felt that this was an unfair action and I chased him right into his home, and continued where we had left off a few minutes ago. This time I was on top of him, but not for very long. Suddenly I felt the sensation of having developed the gift of flying. Furthermore, I was doing it upside down. I soon discovered that it was the tailor who was the force behind my aeronautic talent. He held me upside down for what seemed like an eternity, and admonished me:

'It is not nice for a Jewish boy, who attends cheder, to behave like a *sheigetz*' (derogatory term for a gentile boy). Other than offering me the flying lesson and admonishing me, he never laid a hand on me again. The experience, however, left me in awe of adults, for it was the first time I had been manhandled by one. Reverence filled me, for the man and the home where it took place. Maybe this incident was also responsible for my fear of heights.

Most houses were small, with dirt floors and straw-thatched roofs, with anything from one to three rooms at the most. Ours was in this category. One thing was common to all homes: none of them had any of the basic modern conveniences of the twentieth century. We had wells instead of running water, tubs instead of bathrooms, outhouses instead of toilets and the famous *pripitchek* instead of light bulbs. There is a Yiddish folk song, 'Oyf Dem Pripitchek', which describes a rebbe teaching children the fundamentals of the alphabet by the light and warmth of the *pripitchek*, and I wish to take this opportunity to explain this term. A *pripitchek* (Ukrainian word) was a kind of niche, usually attached to an oven, with an exhaust pipe, and an altar on which kindling wood was burned to provide light in the room. It was very important that the exhaust worked properly because when it malfunctioned, as it frequently did, the carbon monoxide that accumulated produced terrific headaches, retching and vomiting. This phenomenon was known as *farchadet*. For all intents and purposes, Kortiless existed in a different century, and as far as I knew it was very happy with its lot. I know I was. Occasionally I would hear stories of the various wonders that existed in the world. Never did I dream that by the time I had reached the age of 10, I would have discovered its secrets, seen many of its wonders, traveled great distances, seen many different countries and bemoaned the events that drove me away from my Kortiless.

The second picture of Kortiless, which is ingrained upon my mind, is from about a week after our liberation from the Nazi scourge, in the summer of 1944. My family and I were standing on the ashes and rubble of what once had been our house and we had an almost unobstructed view to the other end of the village. Slowly we walked through the village, stopping at every site that was once a Jewish home, while my parents made their parting speeches. I forgave the tailor for manhandling me and I cried for his son, my friend, as I did for many of my other friends. It is difficult to describe and recapture the emotional upheaval, the sensation of bitter loss and the depth of our sorrow as we proceeded with our tour through the village. With the exception of a few Ukrainian villagers who were genuinely pleased to see us and were glad that we had survived the ordeal, most people were openly hostile to us. They were disappointed that not all the Jews of Kortiless were dead. Two adults and two children were all that remained out of a population of about one hundred and fifty Jews.

Our bodies revealed the terrible suffering that we had endured for the past two-and-a-half years, but as for my mind, it was scarred by the blow to my human dignity. Yet the experience taught me that despite great despair, there is always hope, and at a time when the contents of my world had been reduced to emptiness, I continued to believe that there is a God. The final act before leaving Kortiless was conducted by my father, on the site upon which our synagogue once stood. He chanted 'El Maleh Rachamim' (God who is full of mercy) and promised to recite Kaddish (a prayer for the dead) every time that he was praying with a minyan (a group of ten adult men) – a promise that he fulfilled until his dying day.

Reminiscences have no chronological order and memories crystallize through various stimulants. Essentially, the above paragraph describes the end of an odious period in my life, caused by the inhumanity of the 'super race' and the beginning of a new odyssey which was to take me half way around the world. Before I enter into this chamber of my memory bank, however, I shall deal with the events which led my family and me to this point. From my previous description of the physical layout of Kortiless, it will be evident that the Jewish community did not live within the confines of a ghetto, but was interspersed throughout the village and, on the whole, maintained good neighborly relations with the Ukrainians. The village Jew was in many ways a rustic and much more robust than his *shtetl* counterpart. Many of them knew how to till the soil, to handle livestock and even to ride a horse. Jews were officially barred from owning land, at least until the Soviets took over – and then no one could really own it. Arrangements were worked out on a rental basis that managed to circumvent this law. My parents had an arrangement like that, and until I was 4 years old we lived on a farm on the outskirts of Kortiless. I had to attend cheder. My brother, who is two-and-a-half years older than I, lived with my maternal grandparents, but they could not be saddled with the two of us. My parents therefore decided to move to Kortiless.

Most of the Jews there were tradesmen, traders or administrators, and some were *luftmenschen*, who managed to eke out a living by various manipulations. In most cases it was easy to distinguish, by outward appearance, between Ukrainians and Jews. On the other hand, most Jews took pains to learn to speak the language of their host properly, and to write it, to the amazement and envy of the villagers, most of whom were ignorant of this art. In many ways the Jews absorbed and exhibited a gregarious nature like that of their gentile neighbours. At the same time, I must stress the fact that the village Jew was observant and God-loving. A place like Kortiless was not exactly a breeding ground for heretics. Despite the proximity of the people there was only one known case of intermarriage. The man was Jewish and he was labeled the Meshumed (the Destroyer). In case I give the impression of some ideal picture of coexistence, I wish to make it clear that there was anti-Semitism and it was not latent. It was an integral part of life and no one was shocked when it showed its ugly head. The Ukrainian received it with his mother's milk and displayed it with fervor when the

7

occasion arose. There were exceptions, of course, as a rule, in the pecking order of Ukrainian society the *Szyd* (Jew) was on the lowest rung.

There is very little that I remember from the days when we lived on the farm except for two events. The first one is my accidentally acquired skill of horseback riding. I was alone in the house and for some reason I climbed up and sat on the windowsill. One of the horses came over and stood next to the open window. His back was just the right height for me to slip on to it. The minute the horse felt me on his back, however, he moved away from the house, with me as his passenger. I grabbed the horse's mane and held on for dear life, and at the same time screamed my lungs out from fear. Evidently the horse understood this as a sign to quicken his pace, and he began to gallop. Since I did not give him directions, he chose his own course and delivered me to a pasture, about a kilometer away from the house, where other horses were grazing. I still do not know how I managed to stay on, but now that the horse was stationary, the ordeal was less frightening – at least less frightening than trying to jump off. Eventually one of the farmers, who came to pick up his horse from pasture, relieved me of my predicament and delivered me home. It was almost twenty years before I gathered the courage to mount a horse again.

ONE MUST HAVE A GOOD EAR TO ATTEND CHEDER

The other thing that I remember from my days on the farm has to do with the fact that because I was surrounded by Ukrainians, my playmates did not did not speak *mameh loshon* (mother tongue), meaning Yiddish. The result was that I felt more comfortable speaking Ukrainian. Even if I knew Yiddish well enough, I used to slip into Ukrainian occasionally, without realizing it, to the amusement of my family in Kortiless. I found their reaction encouraging and even in my early childhood days, the ham in me would take advantage of this talent. When I first began to attend cheder, I became embroiled in an argument with a boy next to me. He whispered to me that I was a 'goy' (gentile). Since my Yiddish vocabulary lacked enough abrasive words, for the required response to such an accusation, I reverted to Ukrainian. Being angry, I delved into my treasury of foul language, learned from my playmates, and delivered what I thought was a masterly abuse of my classmate. The rebbe was not as amused as my relatives by my talent. In fact for a moment I thought that my ear and I were going to part company. While keeping a firm grip on my ear and twisting it into the shape of a pretzel, the rebbe began to recite the list of sins that I had committed, and he took his time about it. With the same sing-song in his voice as when he explained a passage from the Torah, he said: 'To begin with, you spoke when I did not ask you to. Next, cheder boys do not pick fights like *shkotsim'* (derogatory word for gentile boys). He continued by explaining: 'A cheder [literally a room, a place of study for young boys] is not a marketplace where one speaks Ukrainian while bargaining over the price of a horse. Finally, if I ever hear you use this kind of language again, I will twist both your ears off.' I must mention that each admonition was accompanied by an additional twist of my ear, like a punctuation mark: a special technique that he had developed through years of practice. I was relieved to hear that he was not going to twist my ears off at this moment – but he reserved the privilege for some future date. There was no chance for me to plead my case or argue that I was horribly provoked. The rebbe led me by the ear into a corner and made me face the wall. There was a lesson to be learned from this incident: that you had to have a good ear to attend cheder. The nickname Goy stuck to me for a while.

The rebbe, after hearing my side of the story from my father, tried to make amends by twisting the ear of anyone who called me by that nickname. This intervention by the rebbe on my behalf did not improve my lot, but it improved the tactics and the taunts by my classmates. They would shape the corners of their jackets to resemble a sow's ear and sing a disparaging ditty about goyim. Eventually the name-calling stopped for two reasons. The taunts somehow lost their effect on me and I stopped reacting to them. Secondly, it became evident that I was a diligent student. From the time I started attending cheder, of course, my head was shaved and the only remnantsof my nearly-blond, straight hair were my *peyes* (ear locks), which refused to curl.

A STAR IS BORN

Although to this day I cannot read a note of music, I am blessed with a good ear and a beautiful voice, inherited from my father. This talent did not go unnoticed in our synagogue, which did not possess a cantor but had an abundance of good *baal tfilah*. My father, despite his young age, was at the top of the list (the honor of conducting the services was usually reserved for the older congregates). As I understand it, there was a decided preference in our community for a *baal tfilah* over a cantor. It was felt that whereas the former used the contents of the prayer and his own brand of *nusach* (style), coupled with a passable voice, to produce the right response, the cantor concentrated on the glory of his voice and in the process garbled the words. This was an unfair prejudice, because many wonderful cantors existed. A wandering *baal tfilah* by the name of Velvel der Alter would arrive in our village occasionally, with his son – I imagine that it was for the High Holidays. His renditions, with the help of his son, would produce an emotional catharsis amongst the worshippers. I discovered in later years that although he had his own *nusach*, he had no qualms about also incorporating the melodies of famous cantors. I was fascinated by this man and thrilled by his dramatic renditions, and stayed close to him when he prayed. His melodies easily lingered with me so that I would join in, with confidence, in my soprano voice. The old *baal tfilah* was not oblivious to my contribution and encouraged me to participate, and I eagerly obliged. A star was born. This recognition by 'the Master' placed me in an enviable position amongst my peers and was a source of pride for my relatives.

THERE WAS SINGING AND THERE WAS DANCING
AND A GOOD TIME WAS HAD BY ALL

Music and singing are, to this day, an exciting part of my life. Family gatherings at which my father played the fiddle, and my Uncle Shmilke the mandolin – both of them without formal training – were like an adventure. Most of my family had beautiful voices and sang with abandon and relish in a harmony that could rival choirs. There was a constant supply of new songs to be learned from my Uncle Bentse's record collection, played on an impressive-looking gramophone. Most of those songs, as well as the liturgical melodies, are still part of my repertoire. Holidays were occasions for rejoicing and not only for the observance of a ritual. Each one carried with it a certain decorum but none of them, with the exception of Yom Kippur (Day of Atonement), was solely a solemn occasion. The singing on holidays, of course, was without musical accompaniment and secular songs were not included.

Simcha Torah was my favourite holiday, not only because of the singing during the *hakafot* (dancing with the Torah), in which I took an active part, following the official recognition of my talent by Velvel der Alter; there was also dancing and the additional fun of the mischievous acts which accompanied it. Any prank that would secure a hearty laugh from the congregation, even while the services were in progress, was acceptable and anyone was fair game. It usually revolved around a harmless thing like tying together the *taleissim* (prayer shawls) of a number of worshippers, so that when one of them stood up, he would remove his neighbors' *taless* in the process. It should be understood that the *taleissim*, which only married men wore, were not little prayer shawls but large enough to cover the entire body. A prank like that would cause an entanglement resulting in a great commotion. To

11

accuse the *baal tfilah* of inadvertently omitting a certain portion of the prayer would spark a rebuttal of self-defense until he noticed the smiling faces and realized that he was the victim. He would return to his duties, trying to maintain a solemn expression. Exchanging the places of the men's and the women's overcoats and mixing them up provided an additional touch of humor at the end of the services, when everyone began looking for their coats. The people expected these things to happen during Simcha Torah and when they did, they added to the merriment. No doubt, if a stranger were to observe this kind of behavior he would deem it as childish. Though children primarily initiated these pranks, many adults took part in them as well. To us, it was a custom that enhanced the spirit of the holiday.

All holidays needed preparations and these in no small way contributed to the atmosphere beforehand. In Kortiless we did not have the convenience of going into a supermarket and loading up the cart with all the necessary provisions. Everything that was essential in terms of food, clothing, decorations and other trappings was the product of one's labor. Chanukkah candles had to be made. To begin with animal fat, chelev (lard) had to be secured. The lard of hogs could certainly not be used. The fat was melted in a big pot, outdoors, over a fire. Strings were attached to a stick, dipped into the melted lard and raised. The cold temperature would quickly harden the lard and the process would be repeated until candles of the desired thickness were obtained. These were not multicolored and certainly not dripless or odorless, but their smell was part of the festive aroma to which the fried latkes (potato pancakes) also contributed their share. The crackling noise which the burning candles made served as a percussion accompaniment while father sang the blessings and we joined in for Amen and Ma'oz Tsur Yeshuati. The sounds fitted particularly well to the words of a beautiful Yiddish Chanukkah song: 'Oh you little candles which relate stories ...'. Another way of making Chanukkah candles, which was expensive, was with the use of oil. Five potatoes were cut in half; the bottoms flattened for stability; each potato was hollowed out to make a receptacle for the oil; and a wick was placed in it. The richer Jews used oil, of course, and did not have to resort to makeshift potato *chanukiot*.

The family gathering at my maternal grandparents' home was an exciting affair. My Zeide (Grandpa) Berchik would offer the honor of lighting the beautifully ornate oil *chanukia*, which he brought from America, to my Zeide Meir. Zeide Meir's voice was beautiful and he received amply-qualified help from the family, so the ceremony was impressive, but to me it felt unusually long. Not because of the introduction of additional text, but because right after the ceremony two crucial events took place. The first was 'Chanukkah gelt' (money) and the second was the feast of latkes. How long can one wait, to become a millionaire and taste manna from heaven in the same evening? I had been waiting a whole year for this occasion but when you finally reached the point when your palms were itchy and you were salivating, every moment counted. My brother and I were the only children in the clan. With doting grandparents, uncles and parents our takings for the evening must have been considerable. To tell the truth, the amount was irrelevant because I do not remember ever spending the money. There was no place in Kortiless where I could do so – I could not make purchases at my grandparents' store. Most of the fun lay in the act of receiving and then handling all those coins. Zeide Berchik would put his hand deep into his pocket, make a jangling noise for our benefit, extract a fistful of coins, divide them up and ask us what we would do with all this money. My answer must have been ludicrous because everyone laughed and I received a great bear hug from him. Zeide Meir assumed a sad face and explained that he had changed his pants before he came, and forgotten the Chanukkah gelt. Before my chin reached the floor with disappointment, the coins miraculously appeared. Latke with *smetene* (sour cream) is a treat worth waiting for the whole year. We must have indulged in it on other occasions during the year but it was this particular circumstance which made it so memorable. The sour cream was home-made, most likely unpasteurized and definitely without commercial additives. When I came to Canada I discovered, to my horror, that people ate latkes with applesauce and some even ate them with sugar. Amongst the many other adjustments that I had to make, accepting this eating habit was 'small potatoes'. In the land of Israel I had to accept the fact that latkes, on Chanukkah, played second fiddle to doughnuts filled with a dab of jam. During the course of my narrative, which I am writing about almost a half a century after the events took place, I will be making references to the various dishes that were prepared and consumed as if they were masterpieces of haute cuisine. In fact they were simple and humble but because they were laced with bittersweet memories they were so extraordinarily special.

PESACH: THE HOLIDAY OF SPRING AND FREEDOM

Pesach (Passover) was the holiday that seemed to need most preparation. To begin with, the wheat grain was saved up months in advance. Then as Pesach approached, the Jewish community took over the mill for several days, where under the supervision of one of the elders, the wheat was ground. The flour was delivered directly to the house where the matzos (unleavened bread) were to be baked. A number of homes were designated, whose ovens were to be used for baking of the matzos. Every home had an oven, the kind usually found in bakeries, but the larger ones were chosen. The oven had to be prepared kosher for Pesach and every possible particle of food that could be called chametz (leavened) had to be removed from the vicinity of the baking area. Of course this meant that the routine of the family whose oven was chosen was considerably curtailed for the duration of the baking. I remember that for some reason it was the men who performed the task of baking. The most important element was speed. There was a time limit of

14

eighteen minutes, which must not be exceeded, from the moment the dough was made until the shaped and perforated matzos went into the oven. The amounts were carefully measured and weighed so that each batch of dough exactly fitted the capacity of the oven and there was no danger of leftover dough rising while waiting its turn. I remember running around with two forks in my hands, piercing the rolled-out circles of thin dough, placed on wooden planks like spatulas, that were later inserted into the oven.

The finished product was a sight to behold, for no two matzos were alike in size or shape and would boggle the minds of today's packaging experts. The problem was solved, however, with freshly-washed bed sheets into which the product was dumped, tied up and barricaded from access until the night of the Seder. The worst torture was that we were not even allowed to taste the finished product until the Seder. For some reason, this rule was strictly observed. Preparing the house for Pesach was not just an act of spring cleaning; it verged closer to revamping. After everything was dusted, swept, washed, scrubbed and rearranged, a new layer of a mixture of sand was spread on the dirt floor and packed down by stomping on it. The final result was an impressive transformation. The *bedikat* chametz (checking for leavened particles), which Father would conduct the night before Pesach, seemed superfluous. This was part of the custom, however, and a blessing was made. In order that the blessing should not be in vain, particles of chametz were previously carefully placed in various parts of the house, on pieces of paper. Father, accompanied by us, went around with a candle and a large feather in 'search' of the chametz and scooped it up. The next morning the particles were burned.

There was not a family that did not have to make at least some of the dishes kosher for Pesach. The dishes which were allowed to be koshered had to go through the process of being boiled in a huge caldron, then red-hot irons were immersed, rinsed and finally dunked in running spring water. On the outskirts of the village was a body of water called the Yezre and there the Jewish community would congregate, early in the morning, with their pots and pans, plates and cutlery, to perform the function of koshering their dishes. It was like a picnic. The atmosphere was jovial, with spring in the air and the anticipation of the Seder contributing to the high spirits. At a certain point during the morning, everyone took a break to have the last chametz meal – the last meal until the Seder. Why was it that potatoes boiled in their skins, cabbage borscht and sour pickles tasted so good?

Later in the day, when it became warmer, some of the younger adults and particularly the children would begin dunking themselves as well as the dishes. The few who knew how to swim exhibited what I thought was one of the wonders of human endeavor. I did not know how to swim, but there I was up to my *pupik* (belly button) in water and occasionally dunking myself. One of the horses decided to go for a swim and as he passed close to me his long tail floated by invitingly, and I grabbed it and became seaworthy. This exciting ride did not last for very long. The horse was averse to my idea of fun. To get rid of the little pest who had attached himself to his tail, he kicked out with his hind leg and I went flying. Luckily for me, the horse's legs were in deep enough water to help to reduce the force of the blow that landed on the upper part of my thigh, but it was sufficient to knock the wind out of me. I managed to let out enough of a scream to halt all activity and I became the focus of attention of the entire community. I was the first casualty of the 'Pesach dishes koshering event' and I had a large bruise to prove it. It took me years to get over my shyness of horses.

I AM AN INTEGRAL PART OF THE RITUAL

The Seder, which we celebrated alternately at each grandparents' home, was a special and mysterious event. The rebbe prepared us by constantly repeating the message that 'in every generation, one has to imagine that he himself took part in the exodus from Egypt'. How that was possible was beyond me, because I had never even left Kortiless. But I was certainly eager to play the game and do my part, since I knew that I had a very important role to play. I was the one that was going to ask the Four Questions. It was many years later that I became aware of the theatrical aspect that is present in the Haggadah and takes place in the ritual of the Seder. The three vital elements of theatre – space, actors and audience – are built into the ceremony. Without realizing it then, perhaps I was suffering from the nagging sensation of stage fright, as I diligently studied my part. It was not only a matter of reciting the four crucial questions by heart. In fact I was supposed to leave the impression that I was capable of reading, in Hebrew, from the Haggadah and to prove that I understood the contents. In fact, not just reading but chanting, and at the same time translating; into Yiddish, without losing the rhythm or quality of the melody. I was used to this system from my study of the Chumash (Pentateuch) in the cheder. These were different circumstances, however, because I was to be heard by the experts and by an older brother who was poised to correct me if I faltered. My performance had to be immaculate.

I was grateful that I had two chances to do my stuff. When my turn came, which happened quite early in the proceedings, I gave it my best shot. Not only did I read from the Haggadah but when the time came to translate, I looked into my grandfather's face, and with the help of my hands, an active thumb and rhythmic swaying of my body (a trick I learned from observing my rebbe) I carried it off with aplomb, to the delight of everyone. Success had its price. While I was still busy savoring my moments of glory, my brother planned his strategy of positioning himself closer to my grandfather and snatching the *affikoman,* as Grandfather went to perform the ritual of washing his hands. I could console myself with the fact that when the time came to redeem the *affikoman,* I would not be excluded from the negotiations and would enjoy my share of the prize.

Furthermore, I still had another chance to rectify the situation the following night. I did not succeed of course, because my brother was there before me.

There was one very tense moment for me during the proceedings of the Seder. This was the moment when my grandfather filled the Prophet Elijah's cup to the brim; Grandmother went to open the door, with me at her heels; and everyone was poised for his arrival. No matter how hard I peered into the darkness, I saw no sign of him, although I felt the sensation that something brushed by me. If I had any doubts about Elijah's visit, they vanished when I returned to the table and discovered that his cup was not full to the brim anymore. I gleefully pointed out to my grandfather that there was wine missing from Elijah's cup, meaning that he was here and he drank. The rest of the family, of course, enthusiastically received my discovery, even if my brother did laugh at me. There were other aspects of this event that fascinated me. For one thing, Elijah drank very little. Maybe he did not like the grown-up wine and we should have offered him the sweet raisin wine that I enjoyed? If Elijah is actually a spirit, why do we have to open the door for him?

Grandfather assured me that Elijah liked our wine, but since he has so many homes to visit, he would become as drunk as Lot if he were to finish the entire cup in each house. When he began to explain about opening the door, my brother burst in: 'What do you want him to do, crawl through the window?' That one-liner received a good laugh and my question was forgotten. Many years later I discovered one explanation for this custom of opening the door to welcome the Prophet Elijah. It took root in the Middle Ages, for a very practical reason. It was to show gentile neighbors the inside of the house and prove that the Jews were not engaged in the ritual of sacrificing a Christian child. The irony is evident in the prayer which accompanies the welcome, the moment the door is opened for Elijah: 'Pour out Your wrath upon the nations which do not recognize You ...'. The second mystery was that despite my determination to remain awake until the very end of the proceedings, I would wake in my own bed next morning, without the slightest recall of how I got there.

THE THINGS THAT YOU ARE LIABLE TO READ IN THE BIBLE

In my family, it was Mother who assumed the role of telling us bedtime stories. The source of her tales, however, was not Andersen, the Grimm brothers or Mother Goose – I discovered their existence much later in life, when at the age of 13½ I came to Canada and read them as an aid in acquiring my knowledge of the English language. The material which Mother used was from the Bible: the prophets and the military leadership of Joshua, Gideon and Deborah. I learned about Saul, the first chosen king of Israel, who was 'head and shoulders above all men', and who suffered terribly in consequence of his one act of insubordination. Other stories were about King David's mighty exploits in vanquishing Goliath and other enemies, and how he finally carved out a great Jewish kingdom. She told us about the rivalry between David's children, and the insurgency and death of his son, Absalom. We heard many stories about wise King Solomon and his antagonist, Ashmadai. To obtain their freedom, the Maccabees and Bar Kochba opposed the might of an empire.

Some of this material I also learned in cheder but there was a world of difference in its treatment. The rebbe presented indisputable facts – 'as it stands written', he would say – rendering the heroes without the blemishes of human failing: dry, robot-like and distant creatures. With Mother, however, there was room for comments and questions, which both my brother and I were encouraged to make, and she even deviated from the written text. This kind of treatment exposed the events and heroes in a different light, making them real and allowing for personal involvement in their activities.

'A little knowledge is a dangerous thing', goes the proverbial saying. My little knowledge did not equip me to deal with my rebbe's concept of the scriptures. During my second year of the cheder – it must have been then, because we were studying the book of Genesis and that is avoided with beginners – I lamely expressed my sympathy for Terach, whose idols were smashed by his son, Abraham. I thought that the rebbe would use his reserved privilege to twist off my ears on the spot. For some reason he did not do that but instead went into a lengthy tirade about his wasted effort to 'beat Torah' into my classmates' empty heads and mine. We were nothing but habitual sinners, with me at the head of the class, and it was 'due to your misdemeanors and to your heads stuffed with straw, of course, that the arrival of the Messiah is being delayed.' That was an awful responsibility to bear on 5-year-old shoulders. The fear of God was systematically instilled in the cheder. The rebbe made sure to point out our human frailty, imperfection and susceptibility to sin, and warned us of the day of retribution. Then came the clincher: he warned us that although we were the perpetrators of sins, they were attributable to Father's account without his being aware of it. I must admit that this arrangement pained my conscience and bothered me more than the fear of retribution. I really did not think that I was such a habitual sinner.

Some things were clearly put: 'On Shabbes (Sabbath) you do not whistle.' Not that whistling was encouraged during the week, but at least it was tolerated by some. 'On Shabbes you do not skate.' Not that I had any skates. But you did not even run and glide on your heels on an available stretch of ice. 'You do not dirty your Shabbes clothes.' Not that I even purposely dirtied my weekday clothes. In brief, there was a bunch of 'don'ts' and a bunch of 'dos' and occasionally I became confused between them. Result: sin. Today, I can freely admit that the transgressions which drove the rebbe into long tirades were not due to innocence or ignorance, but purposely designed by us to goad him, because his tirades were more interesting than the lessons. Possibly this is where the first seeds of my rebellious nature were planted.

My Ukrainian playmates and friends had their great heroes: Chmelnitzki, Petlura, Bulba and some others of whom they were very proud and whom they tried to emulate. They bragged about their heroic struggle to free the Ukrainians from the yoke of Polish rule and abuse. That may have been true but in the wake of that struggle the primary target was the Jews and in that process, these great heroes had taken innumerable Jewish lives and destroyed many communities. I could not present them with this grievance, for the sake of my health, and instead offered to tell them a story of my favorite hero. I told them the story of David and Goliath.

Evidently they were impressed with its contents and must have repeated it to some adult or the priest. Several days later they came back and as a reward for my efforts to contribute to their enlightenment, they knocked me to the ground and humiliated me for having the gall to tell them a story from the *Biblia* and claiming that King David was Jewish.

TRADITION, TRADITION

Lag B'Omer was a holiday that enhanced my Jewish pride. I played the role of a Jewish soldier and one of my uncles made sure that I had a bow and arrows to qualify me properly for this role. My heart went out to Bar Kochba and the betrayal he suffered by his allies which brought about his eventual defeat, but at the same time I was proud of him, because despite the odds against him, he was not afraid to fight. The greatest part of the holiday was the bonfire around which all the younger people gathered to sing and hear words of wisdom and encouragement to help us carry on with our own lives. Having a bonfire symbolizing a national Jewish event may seem like nothing much to write about, were it not for the fact that this was during the time when the Russians occupied our part of the Ukraine, and an event like that was not something they treated lightly. They categorically forbade any activity that was not Russian in its intent and origin. Indeed, the Jewish section of the Communist Party was vehemently opposed to anything that had to do with Judaism, and they were holier than the Pope in their efforts to stem it. Although the section advocated Jewish rights, like those of other minorities in the Soviet Union, in order to develop the Yiddish culture, they fought Hebrew as if it was an enemy to its progress. In the educational institutions and newspapers, which were anti-religious, Hebrew words were systematically eradicated from the lexicon and those words that were rooted in the Yiddish language were purposely misspelled beyond recognition. A Zionist, to them, was someone who not only advocated the weakening of the Soviet Union by encouraging leaving it, but also a traitor who allied himself with imperialist Britain. This event, therefore, which was organized by a clandestine Zionist organization named Gordonia, was a testament to Jewish ingenuity and enterprise. It was cloaked as a youth activity to honor a freedom fighter who gave his life for principles that were close to the heart of Mother Russia. Dressed in their Pioneer and Comsomol uniforms, Jewish youths of Kortiless were paying tribute to Father Stalin, with the heritage of Bar Kochba in their hearts.

POLISH RULE IS ON THE DECLINE

I can recall several events that signaled the end of Polish domination. To begin with there was the hoarding of food. We did not have any canned articles, but there were ways of treating some foods so that they would last for a long time. Bread was baked in larger quantities than usual, sliced and dried in the oven. The only way it was possible to eat it afterwards was to soak it in liquid, because it was as hard as a rock, but it never became moldy and if it was kept safely from rodents, it sustained life. Years later, when I reached the western world, I saw people eating toast as if it were a great delicacy, and I could not understand why they were doing it when there was fresh bread available. I usually avoided eating toast, perhaps because it reminded me of the past, and when I did indulge in it, the crumbs would cause me to cough.

THE UKRAINIAN FARMERS' FUN AND GAMES

Those Poles who were Roman Catholics were not opposed to the religious practices of the Ukrainians, who are Pravoslavni. Sundays, therefore, were special days on which to observe our Ukrainian hosts in action. They gathered from many miles around Kortiless, attired in their colorful costumes and wearing new *postelee* on their feet. The farmers did not own shoes: instead they wore *postelee* which were woven from birch bark. After the foot was wrapped in a rag, the *postelee* was put on and fastened with a string through hooks that were part of its structure. Every Sunday a new pair was made for the occasion. The Jews of Kortiless started their services earlier than usual so as not to meet up with the invading hordes. It was accepted and understood that it was healthier for Jews not to be in the street before and after the Ukrainian services took place. The services were intended for the purification of the souls of believers, but there were also those who believed that this was a good opportunity to settle old grievances. There was never a Sunday without a scrap between some factions or individuals, or someone baiting some helpless Jew who inadvertently crossed their path and became the focus of their religious zeal. Usually no real bodily harm came to him, but he served as a target for settling a 'very old score', and would be abused and humiliated for being a 'Christ-killer'. For my paternal grandmother, Sunday was an unusually busy day because she was the healer of the area. For the record, I do not wish to leave the impression that the Ukrainians were all drunken brawlers, because for the most part their Sundays were devoted to social engagements, including visiting Jewish friends. Many of them came to visit my parents, and included my mother in the conversation because they considered her a *'chitraya Szydovka'* (a wise Jewess) and therefore made an exception in her case. They also accepted the fact that she did not join them in drinking the *samagon* (a powerful home brew) which my father made and kept for these occasions, in order to bolster the spirits and make the conversation flow. After war broke out, however, Sunday became like a regular day, with very little attendance in church.

The Ukrainian farmers had a kind of a ritual at the end of a day's work in their fields. One of them would begin to sing and the rest would join in the chorus. It was a kind of haunting melody that remained the same, but most of the words would change each day. Each time, a different singer would make up a verse, dealing with the events of the day, or telling some ribald story in rhyme, and the singers would head for home to the rhythm of the song. To my childish imagination, it was as if they were singing a lullaby to the sun, for it soon went to sleep in the goyish cemetery.

THE INVASION OF THE MONSTER

My most exciting and still very vivid memory of the Russian–German invasion of Poland was my first sight of a motor vehicle. I was playing with some friends, near my house, when I noticed a huge cloud of dust approaching the village, accompanied by the frightening drone of the motor. Never had I seen anything move so fast on the ground, although for the past few days I had seen many aircraft. When it drew close enough for me to notice the grill and the headlights, it looked like some threatening monster with bared fangs and glaring eyes. Out of sheer fear – and maybe out of reluctance of showing it – all of us stayed frozen to the spot and we waited until the thing had passed us. Then we took off after it in a delighted frenzy. No creature in Kortiless who saw this remarkable apparition, remained indifferent to it. Chickens, caught off guard on the road, cackled as they tried frantically to resume their lost art of flying, in their effort to avoid being trampled. Cows in nearby pastures became so confused by this noisy intrusion that they began to prance around, mooing and clumsily kicking out their hind legs, while the horses, loudly neighing, stampeded. The dogs, thinking that this was something into which they could really sink their teeth, were at the lead, chasing and barking, followed at breakneck speed by a shouting group of younger people. I was not the only one who had never seen a car in his life, judging from the crowd which gathered around it when it stopped in front of my grandfather's home.

As I reached the car, I saw my Uncle Yerachmiel come out of the house, dressed in his Polish NCO uniform, with a bag in his hand, saying goodbye to my grandparents. I ran towards him and he lifted me in his arms and gave me a big hug, but instead of setting me down, as I expected him to do, he carried me inside the car. The car turned around and I was driven all the way home. I thought that my heart would explode from excitement and pride in my uncle. How did he know exactly what I wanted? There was no doubt in my mind that with heroes like my uncle, the war would be over in no time, and that he would teach Hitler a lesson.

Several weeks later my uncle returned from the war, in the middle of the night, but without his uniform, which he had traded in for civilian clothes while making his way home. It was not exactly wise to fall into Russian hands wearing a Polish uniform. He spoke scornfully of the Polish cavalry on horseback, fighting the might of the German tanks as if they were Cossacks. There was no sympathy for the Poles who were massacred, but grave concern for the millions of Jews who fell into German hands. According to the stories which were circulating, about the terrible treatment of Jews under German occupation, it sounded as if Chmelnitzki or Petlura were benign gentlemen compared to Hitler. In fact the Polish government, especially after Marshal Pelsudski died, did sympathize with the Jewish policies of the Nazis and implemented many of them to get rid of Jews, despite Poland having signed an international agreement, which obligated her to care for her minorities. The government of Poland adopted a policy that was simple and evil – a throwback to the dark ages – by ceasing any aid to the Jewish community, hindering its development in any way possible and demanding all taxes due.

AND THEN THE RUSSIANS CAME

The Russians came to Kortiless and the general opinion was that it 'was good for the Jews', despite the fact that the Russians were now allies of the Germans. In this case an exception was made and we befriended 'the friend of my enemy'. How good it was for the Jews remained to be seen, but for me it was certainly good. My three uncles were all at home. Ever since I could remember, my uncles came home for special occasions, like holidays, and then would go away again: Uncle Yerachmiel to the army, Uncle Bentse to his teaching position somewhere and Uncle Shmilke to his place of study in some faraway city. This time, however, they were back to stay for good. As I remember my uncles, they were a special breed of people because they always did original things with me that I liked, never scolded me, yet rarely spoiled or pampered me.

Uncle Yerachmiel, who possessed some skill in communications, was soon tipped by the Soviets for an important administrative position in a big city, which he gladly assumed. Occasionally he would come to visit, bringing presents and stories about life in the big city and especially about the Jewish community under the new Soviet administration. The most exciting news was his announcement that from now on, due to his efforts, Kortiless would have a telephone. I must admit I was not aware what this meant and what the excitement was all about. Despite my uncle's explanation that he would be able to speak to me from great distances with the aid of a wire, I remained skeptical and believed that this was too great a feat even for him, until one day I actually heard his voice from the instrument I was holding to my ear. We did not have these instruments at home, of course, and this event took place at Uncle Shmilke's office. I automatically assumed that my two uncles were playing a trick on me. After a thorough search of the premises, and persuaded by my mother who had taken me there for the purpose of this conversation – I was finally convinced that I had actually spoken to my Uncle Yerachmiel on the telephone and I became a convert to the wonders of modern scientific accomplishments. After all, I was already an experienced car traveler.

Uncle Shmilke returned from his studies (which he could not complete because the place was now under German occupation) in the company of an elegant and wealthy Polish–Jewish couple, who were his friends and unexplainably still in possession of a huge motor vehicle. The man was a real doctor and somehow must have obtained the authority, through the proper connections, to retain the vehicle and his other possessions. They eventually moved on but left my uncle a huge gray dog and a bicycle. Either one was enough to fill the heart of a little boy with sheer joy, and I can still relish the thrill of the many rides, sitting on the bar, with the comforting warmth of my uncle's breath on my neck, and the gigantic dog chasing us. It is not a childish illusion about the size of the dog, because I remember, when we both faced each other, we were nose to nose.

Owing to his education, even though it was in the field of science, Uncle Shmilke became the official administrator, a kind of commissar, of the village of Kortiless. This great honor and appointment were not awarded without a price to pay. Even if by that time, twenty years after the revolution, some of the measures initiated to safeguard its gains were more relaxed, they were still sternly applied to those who were in ther direct service of the state. To the Russians, all religions were suspected of affiliation with the former regime, and counter-revolutionary. Synagogues as well as churches, therefore, were closed; religious activitiesy such as teaching the Bible were halted; the offices of rabbi or priest were abolished; worship was banned; and the six-day work-week made the observance of the Sabbath impossible. It is true that all legal aspects of inequality between Jew and Gentile were officially abolished: in fact it was officially forbidden for Ukrainians to address a Jew by the derogatory term *Szyd* and they had to use the more enlightened Russian name, *Yivrey*. For my uncle, who was always a religious man, this theoretically meant that he had to formally renounce religion and become a member of the Communist Party.

No such formal renunciation ever took place, however, but my uncle received his job with the tacit agreement that he would be a staunch and loyal party member. He had to curb his openly-religious activities, but at home he continued to observe. Every morning before going to work, he would say his prayers and carefully remove the telltale signs of the tefillin (phylacteries) from his left arm. Because religious articles were impossible to obtain, and in order to atone for his feeling of guilt about having to hide his Jewish activity, he meticulously copied, in his beautiful handwriting, the contents of a prayer book and spent much time secretly fixing the frayed pages of others. This handcrafted prayer book remained in my father's possession during the terrible years in the forest. Today there is one page left, enclosed in a glass frame, standing on my brother's desk in his law office.

I HAVE PULL AT SCHOOL

Uncle Bentse became the principal of the local school. The former principal fled – a Pole by origin and a flagrant anti-Semite, who used a system of long suspensions for the smallest infractions, real or imaginary, to limit participation of Jewish students. I was too young to attend regular school but looked forward to it and the special status that it would grant me because my uncle was the principal. My brother, however, who attended school, claimed that for him it did not make any difference, and that he hardly saw Uncle Bentse, nor did my uncle offer him any preferential treatment. There are many things that I remember about Uncle Bentse: his greenhouse, where he grew all kinds of vegetables and flowers; his black-and-white dog by the name of Medyush; the riddles and games he would play with me, even if some of the riddles contained numbers that I had difficulty understanding. But the most fascinating things were his impressive gramophone and his record collection of music and songs, which were an inexhaustible source of secular and even cantorial songs for many of our family gatherings. One day, a new teacher by the name of Tanya arrived. She was a Russian Jewess and a very pretty lady, and somehow I found out that she would become my aunt. I did have an aunt (who was married to my deceased Uncle Moshe-David) whom I rarely saw because she lived in faraway Ratno. Tanya was different in her manners, her dress, her speech and in the fact that she did not speak a word of Yiddish, and knew very little about her heritage. She was immersed in a crash course because conditions in Kortiless dictated this kind of absorption, and within a very short time she not only spoke Yiddish but had become aware of Jewish customs and religion. I learned Russian from her – a simple transition because in most cases the difference from Ukrainian is based on dialect and the secrets of the Cyrillic alphabet. Essentially, it can be said that despite the official denouncement of the evils of religion and the limitations imposed on it, Jewish life in Kortiless flourished and was bolstered by the sense of equality that was accorded by the Soviets. Kortiless was too small a community to have any contrary impact on the scheme of Russian policy; besides the occasional indoctrination meetings, conducted by some political functionary, and pamphlets which were distributed, depicting grotesque caricatures of the ugly capitalists abusing the working class, life for everyone continued unhindered.

THE CROSS IN THE HEEL INCIDENT

Since Kortiless never had an official rabbi, there was no such position to dispose of. The shochet continued with his ritual slaughter because, after all, no Jew had the heart to kill his pet chicken or cow with his own hand. At the same time Jewish children continued to pay 'social calls' on the rebbe and 'taste' his wife's delicious cookies, which we actually never saw. All children had to join the Pioneer or Comsomol youth groups, according to their age.

Even though the church and synagogue were to stay officially closed, they continued to function, but it was evident that the church suffered a more severe setback. One particular incident, which caused great furor and controversy amongst Christians, had to do with a new shipment of shoes that came from the Soviet Union. 'Shoes for the farmers instead of *postelee*' was another 'stride forward' in the name of the great revolution. Mother Russia just loved to use the term, 'a stride forward' – maybe this way she never realized how backward she was. Someone had discovered that the heel of these shoes was not made of one solid piece but was hollow and contained a cross that supported it. An accusing finger was pointed at the Jews, of course, who were supposedly behind this evil scheme to humiliate the cross. My uncle had his hands full trying to allay tempers, and enlisted the aid of the priest, for the price of offering his son the position of assistant in charge of police affairs. The priest tried to explain that there was no anti-religious motive behind cross imbedded in the heel, but only the dictates of production. The shoes nevertheless had to be shipped back to wherever they came from and the farmers continued wearing their *postelee*.

BREST LITOVSK IS THE SOURCE OF NEW TIDINGS

I was born with a tiny white spot on the pupil of my right eye. There were all kinds of reasons why I did not receive medical attention, amongst them the lack of a doctor's referral, and travel restrictions for Jews during Polish occupation. The Russians changed all that. A doctor who made routine visits to various villages examined me and decided that I had to see an eye specialist in Brest Litovsk. How can I best describe the excitement that filled my heart when I discovered that I was going to make this trip with my mother? I imagine that Columbus really would have understood me, because I was about to discover the world beyond Kortiless. The trip started out with the usual transportation available, a horse and wagon. After almost a day of being cooped up in the wagon, my initial excitement was beginning to abate and I wished I was back in Kortiless.

Finally we reached a town which had a train station, and many hours of waiting began, during which I assumed that somewhere a plot was being hatched to prevent me from reaching my destination. When the train rolled into the station, its locomotive was decorated with red flags and a huge picture of Lenin, the father of the revolution. I was in awe of this emblem of power and assumed that the glorious stories I had heard about Lenin and Stalin were true.

I really had no idea what to expect in Brest Litovsk. Everything I encountered was for me a new experience, to which I was subjected in a most compressed and concentrated manner. Everything was so overwhelming that I began to expect, every minute, something new to happen. To begin with, this was my first ride on a train. After becoming accustomed to the enormous size of the cars and the excitement when the train started to move, I glued my face to the window and watched, with my one good eye, as new wonders appeared and were quickly left behind. I discovered that a certain section of the window, owing to a fault in the glass, had a distorting effect on objects. I then assumed, of course, that it was part of the magic and converted, at will, to Lilliputian size anything that I viewed through that section of the windowpane, such as cows, houses and people. It began to grow dark outside, and when I turned away from the window I was amazed to discover that the compartment was bathed in light, without a visible *pripitchek* in sight. Mother explained that it was due to electricity; I really did not care what they called it, but it certainly worked better then the *pripitchek*. In Brest they used the same electricity, not only to light up the homes and even the streets, but for many other purposes as well. For instance, it lifted the elevator in the hospital. It was amazing enough to see tall buildings – in Kortiless even the church was only one story high – but an elevator was something that defied imagination. Electricity was the magic word and I was anxious to see what it looked like but I was told, laughingly, by my mother's cousin that this was impossible, and he added that it was very dangerous. It was also very confusing and it took many years for me to clear up this mystery. Despite all the wonders and magic of the modern world, some things could not be altered. After many visits to the eye doctor, with instruments, lights and medication – which eventually caused me to dread these sessions – he finally announced the white spot on my pupil would remain. Although Mother took it to heart, I was not in the least upset. After all, my white spot was responsible for my trip to Brest Litovsk.

ILL WINDS BLOW FROM BREST LITOVSK

It seemed that Mother was concerned not only about the fact that nothing was done to treat my eye, but also about the news of Nazi expansion all over Europe. Brest Litovsk was on the border between Russia and Germany and it contained many Jewish refugees from Poland and various west European countries. Despite the pact with Germany, Russia adhered to at least one humanitarian course of action in maintaining an open border and permitting Jews and other nationals, who managed to reach it, to escape the Nazi scourge – on the condition, of course, that they registered as Russian citizens. The ones who refused the offer were shipped like cattle to various Gulags in Siberia.

Mother spoke to these refugees and their opinion was that nothing could stop the Nazis, and that sooner or later they would invade Russia as well. This is the kind of thinking which never dawned on the Jewish people of Kortiless. It was ridiculous to think that anyone could threaten the might of Russia, who had decimated Poland within a couple of weeks and had just won a glorious victory over Finland. That was Russian propaganda speaking and it did not reveal the fact that she played the role of the hyena. The great (Germany) beast was allowing her to lick a few bones, permitting her to enjoy the morsels to allay her fears, and at the same time planning to return to reclaim the carcass, and in the process inflict a mortal blow. Unfortunately, the people of Kortiless as well as the rest of Russia were prevented from discovering the events that were shaping the world (perhaps ignorance was bliss). What they were told was that Mother Russia was marching *'v'syegda pyerod* [ever forward]) in the footsteps of the great revolution.' She was so busy 'marching forward' that she never looked up or to the sides. In the summer of 1941, when the Nazis invaded Russia, she was so busy 'running backwards' that inside about six months the Germans were thirty kilometers from Moscow and within the cities of Leningrad and Stalingrad. When Russia finally went on the offensive it took her almost a year to drive the Germans back a hundred kilometers from Moscow.

THE NAZI PLAGUE INVADES OUR LIVES

As a child I had experienced the sensations of fear, sometimes with reason and sometimes because of imagined dangers. I had also learned, through the systematic teaching and preaching of the rebbe, the fear of God. I will never forget the fear that I experienced the day that Nazi troops chose, for some reason, to ride through the village of Kortiless. The Ukrainian people cheered them, while the Jews stood by cowed, in shock and in terrible anticipation of the fate that would befall them. The dust-covered soldiers did not look like mortals. The stern expressions on their faces conveyed complete disregard of and disdain for our existence; they did not even acknowledge us with a wave of the hand, but held firmly onto their rifles. It must have been at that moment that I realized this was an era when the forces of evil were triumphant and God was powerless to intervene. Why else would He permit Hitler's messengers, the embodiment of power and evil, to reach Kortiless? There was no doubt in my heart that the force of evil was victorious and this force was to be feared, whereas God was to be loved. The emotion of fear could not be attributed to God because He was our only hope. This was the concept that shaped my attitude towards God and may have been in part responsible, in later years, for my deviation from the path of remaining a religious Jew.

THE REIGN OF TSAR KOLYA THE ABOMINABLE

It did not take long for the Jews of Kortiless to feel the impact of the Nazi occupation. The priest's son, Kolya, whom my Uncle Shmilke was coerced into appointing as chief policeman during the 'cross in the heel crisis', simply changed uniforms. He served his new master with an inhuman ferocity. This man, who for many years had posed as a friend, was aided from childhood in his scholastic efforts by my uncle and my mother. This man, who was once accepted into the circles of Jewish social activity and Jewish homes, became the nemesis of the Jewish community overnight, and bitter antagonist of my uncle and everyone associated with him.

During the course of the Russian occupation, while Kolya served in the capacity of policeman, he behaved obsequiously towards my uncle and showed preferential treatment towards the Jews, to the point where he would arrest a man for insulting a Jew by calling him a *Szyd*. My uncle would curb this overzealous activity and, as a rule, maintained a low profile as administrator. During political rallies, he encouraged Kolya to sit on the podium and sometimes deliver speeches that my uncle wrote for him. This kind of arrangement served my uncle well because it saved him from mouthing platitudes in which he did not believe, displayed the congenial cooperation which existed between Jew and Gentile, and above all made Kolya proud of the honor bestowed upon him. Kolya was a vain, stupid and, as it turned out, evil man.

The edicts limiting the freedom, rights and movements of

the Jews were many. The means whereby they were to be isolated and identified were clear and strict. In big cities it was generally the Germans themselves who took the steps to institute these procedures, whereas in villages they depended on their Ukrainian cohorts to perform their will. In many villages, Ukrainian henchmen implemented Nazi rules, but with a certain amount of restraint. This was not the case in Kortiless. Kolya eagerly adopted every edict, to which he added humiliating wishes of his own and made sure that everything was followed to the letter. As far as I know he did not murder anyone, but was directly responsible for initiating actions that led to the demise of many Jews and Ukrainians, including my Uncle Shmilke.

Kolya became the symbol of ultimate power in Kortiless. One of his first acts, after instituting himself in my uncle's former office, was to send two of his thugs, in the middle of the night, to arrest my uncle. He held him for many hours, while he read to him the speeches which he had delivered as my uncle's assistant, as proof that my uncle was a communist. These speeches had remained in his possession, although when war broke out, my uncle had wisely taken precautions to destroy all possible documents. My uncle did not deny the fact that he worked as an administrator for the Russians and in that capacity employed Kolya as his assistant. Kolya repaid my uncle for that kindness with bone-breaking blows. Yet my uncle stood his ground by denying that he was ever a communist. He admitted he had written the speeches but denied having ever delivered them. The evil Kolya knew that these were the facts and that he had exhausted the subject. There was no more satisfaction for him in the 'interrogation'.

This encounter ended with a terrible beating. Kolya was aided by the two thugs, who then brought my uncle, in a semi-conscious state, and flung him, like a sack of potatoes, at my grandparents' door. The news of my uncle's beating ran like a fearful shudder through the Jewish community and left everyone bewildered at the merciless act of yesterday's 'friend'. I was allowed to visit my uncle, several days after the incident, and my heart ached from sympathy at seeing him in this condition. I cried in outrage that Kolya could inflict such beastly punishment on my uncle. I suggested that we set the dog on Kolya but my uncle laughed and told me that the best thing was to try to avoid Kolya. Mother did not think so, and she went to speak to him, assuming that there was some spark of decency in the man, to which she could appeal. Kolya denied having laid a finger on my uncle, and as punishment for her audacity in accusing him of such an act, he ordered her to come in every day to do menial chores around the building. Mother performed this task for a long time, even on Shabbat, silently enduring abuse and derision all the while. Finally he got tired of this game of abuse and baiting and told Mother that she had served her punishment. At least during this period he left my uncle alone.

It was like a nightmare, except that we were awake and constantly aware it was happening. One of Kolya's most debasing acts was to enter the synagogue, accompanied by his thugs, during Shabbat services. He would make the congregation stand up with bowed heads and humiliate the elders of the community by pulling their beards and making insulting remarks. During his rounds, he and his henchmen would purposely drop prayer books to the ground and, laughing uproariously, kick anyone who bent down to pick them up. This tour of torment ended at the podium, where the Torah was read. With a scornful sneer, Kolya spat in the direction of the worshippers and loudly uttered profanities, before exiting to the ear-splitting laughter of his hyena-like thugs. To avoid being subjected to this abuse and sacrilege, it was decided that only those who had to pray in a minyan should come to the synagogue and everyone else should pray in their homes. Soon Kolya got tired of this game as well, in part because of the intervention of his father (the priest) and for a while the community returned to conducting services.

Like all maniacs, Kolya had periods of relative sanity during which life would become bearable. Then, when a new and original thought of torment occurred to him, he would once again reveal his black soul. The next time it was official business. In order to isolate and identify Jewish homes, a big yellow Star of David had to be affixed prominently to them. All adults had to attach one to the front and one to the back of their outer garments. Kolya chose to personally supervise this task at my paternal grandparents' home, in order to goad and berate my uncle as he was 'decorating' the house with the yellow Star of David. One of the thugs opened the door and was greeted with a deep but loud growl from my uncle's big dog. This gave Kolya a new idea. He told my uncle to bring out the dog and attach two stars to it as well. When the thugs' satanic laughter had subsided, Kolya suddenly announced that it was forbidden for Jews to own pets, because Jews were the lowest form of animal. It was his decision, therefore, to rescue the poor animal from this degrading situation. When he tried to take the dog, it growled and was ready to attack him, but my uncle intervened. Seeing that he could not take the dog without being attacked, he told my uncle to bring it to his house, about two hundred meters away, next to the church, and tie it up. My uncle did as he was told.

Several times the dog managed to escape and return to my uncle, and he had to bring it back. On one occasion, before he had a chance to return the dog, Kolya appeared, pulled out his revolver and shot it right at the doorstep. I was still sick at heart over the senseless loss of that beautiful animal, which I loved, when my own pet suffered the same fate. It was still during the Russian occupation that my Uncle Shmilke brought me a most unexpected gift, something that any child would adore – a beautiful little brown puppy dog. This puppy came from the priest, Kolya's father, who had a bitch. I was not allowed to keep the puppy in the house and my father made an enclosure outside, where it was kept. The bitch discovered the puppy, reclaimed it and brought it back to her burrow underneath the church. I was understandably upset and anxious to get it back as soon as possible. For some reason

I decided to take matters into my own hands, and without telling anyone I went to reclaim it, knowing that it was a dangerous thing to do. From a safe distance, I observed the burrow for a while and then noticed the dog come out and run in the direction of the priest's house. This was my chance. Without any delay, I ran over, crawled under the church, found my puppy and began my retreat. There was enough time for me to straighten up and begin to run a few steps, when the dog appeared. Luckily she was not a big dog but then neither was I big or wise. Instead of setting down the puppy and escaping, I tried to run with it. The puppy howled, the dog growled and I screamed. I put out my hand to protect myself and the dog grabbed my wrist and bit into it. This increased the volume of my screaming by a considerable number of decibels. It was Kolya who came to my rescue and carried me to my grandmother for treatment, and he did not forget to bring along the puppy. I still have a little scar caused by the dog, on my right wrist, to remind me of the incident. But the scar that Kolya left on my young mind a short time later can never heal and never be forgotten.

Jewish commercial life came to a virtual standstill, to the point where it became a severe problem to obtain food. The community organized itself to the best of its ability to help its members. Tradesmen managed to find work but were obliged to receive only a pittance for their labor, so as not to be accused of overcharging, an accusation which would automatically result in dire punishment. Many Jews, including my parents, hired themselves out as farm laborers in return for some food. Jewish homes were ransacked, with the excuse of requisitioning articles that were essential to the German war effort. Brass, copper, bronze and any other metal objects like doorknobs and handles were taken away. My grandfather's centrifugal pump, a source of livelihood, was taken away as a valuable article for the war effort. The things which caused the most pain were the religious objects, like wine cups, chanukiot, Havdalah cups and other family heirlooms that were confiscated. Most of these articles did not go any further than the homes of our Ukrainian neighbors.

One day, when my parents were away working on a farm, I was playing with my dog in front of my house. The dog was about fifty meters away from me, chasing something that I had thrown for him, when suddenly a shot rang out and I heard a yelp. My dog ran back to me, whining, then suddenly keeled over. His body began to shake and then lay still at my feet. I heard the cruel laughter of the Ukrainian policeman who had shot him, and the warning that the next bullet would be for a Jew. I sat beside the corpse of my pet until it became rigid and cold, without even the strength to cry. My brother tried to drag me away but I refused to budge until my parents returned towards evening. When I saw the condition that they were in, the sorrow I felt for my dead pet became meaningless. My parents had been brutally beaten by Ukrainian policemen, when they were caught carrying food which had been given to them for their long day's labor; they were accused of stealing it from the farmers.

Kolya confronted my Uncle Shmilke and told him that he was confiscating his bicycle in the name of the Free Ukrainian State. That was a new twist, but my uncle avoided becoming involved in a conversation on the subject. At the appointed hour he delivered the bicycle to the police station and was ready to leave when Kolya stopped him. Kolya's delusions of grandeur had no limits as he began to boast about the steps that he had been taking towards the establishment of a Ukrainian state. The gist of it was that his policemen were actually paramilitary men, who would one day claim the promise made to them by the Germans, and he, Kolya, might even become the minister of police in the Ukrainian state. He was in a benevolent frame of mind and added that he would take care of the Jews; no harm would come to them. My uncle thanked him for this kind thought but refrained from telling him that he was an evil, unpredictable, black-hearted villain. Not only did the Jews hate Kolya, but he also managed to gain the enmity of many Ukrainians because of his brutality, stupidity and corruption.

His sudden nationalistic fervor and dreams of his own glory gained him the nickname of Tsar Kolya.

A LIFE AND DEATH EXERCISE

It was very early on a Saturday morning, that we heard the roar of motors. By then the village was completely surrounded by German soldiers, who began, quickly and systematically, to evacuate every Jewish adult and march them through the village, to the big circle in front of the church. The children were left behind, in the care of soldiers posted near each Jewish home. This was the first time that I had seen German soldiers at such close proximity without dire consequence; there were two, one near our house and one near our neighbor. My brother and I peeked at them from behind the door and one of them motioned to us come out. His intention was clear and we had no choice but to come out, anticipating the worst. For us the personification of evil was Kolya and we knew that the Germans were even worse.

This was generally true, but not in the case of these two soldiers. Slowly and haltingly we approached, and then I saw one remove the rifle from his shoulder. Assuming that this was it, I grabbed on to my brother and cried out. The soldier, realizing our fear, searched in his pocket and came out with something which he smilingly waved at us. For me, this act of human kindness and the fact that I was still breathing the air was sweeter than the candy that he offered us. Nevertheless, it served the purpose of allaying our fears and soon our neighbor's sons, my friends, Yankele and Itche, joined us. Under these circumstances and at closer range, the soldiers did not seem to be as frightening as when I first saw them drive through our village. They were not larger than life. In fact one of them was chubby, and shorter than my father, and both of them looked older than him. They were doing most of the talking, and because of our Yiddish and the addition of sign language we were able to understand most of what they were saying. To my surprise they expressed sympathy for our plight and told us not to worry about our parents; this time nothing would happen to them. I inspected them closely, their uniforms and their insignia, and I even touched the rifle, but what jarred my senses most was the belt buckle with the skull. There was writing on it, which of course I could not read, and I asked the soldier what it said. *'Gott mit uns'* (God is with us), he obligingly read to me. The words are almost identical to Yiddish, so I fully understood the meaning and my instinct, which I controlled, was to scream at the travesty being perpetrated by these murderers in taking God's name in vain. I comforted myself in the belief that it was not the 'merciful God in heaven' to whom they referred but a heartless god of their own creation, who served their evil purpose. The situation was ironic: four little Jewish children were being cared for and amused by two German soldiers, who would just as easily shoot them, once the order was given to do so. Yet I have always remembered these two soldiers as kind human beings who were swallowed up by a system which denied them human qualities, at least as far as Jews were concerned.

The adults did not fare so well. They were all lined up, facing three machine guns and many soldiers. The officer demanded to know who was the spokesman for the Jewish community. Since Kortiless never had such a position, there was a delay in the reply and no one stepped forward to claim that role. Losing his patience, the officer barked an order to the soldiers manning the machine guns and they fired a volley over the heads of the people. Terror-stricken, everyone screamed and fell to the ground. A man, who was admiringly given the name the Besht by the community, stepped forward. In a loud voice which soothed people's fear, he asked the officer's pardon for the delay and begged him to accept him as the spokesman for the community, despite the fact that he was never officially delegated to that position. The officer scornfully accused him of cowardice, stupidity and trying the patience of a German officer. The Besht humbly agreed that the officer was correct in his accusation but hoped he could still be of service to him. No matter what the Besht said, the officer reinterpreted the words and provided them with a derogatory meaning in order to upbraid and ridicule him. Then he told the Besht to give him one good reason why he should spare the lives of the community. This brought a gasp of fear from the Jews – a response that the officer evidently enjoyed. It was clear that whatever answer the Besht gave, the officer would apply his own judgment, standing there smiling maliciously and tapping his foot. The Besht replied that he was under the impression that the man was a good officer and soldier; his actions would depend on the orders that he had received. Whatever effect this reply had on the officer, he did not reveal it but this time he did not respond with any disparaging remarks. He stopped smiling, walked back a few paces, then gathered his junior officers around him and conducted a lengthy discussion with them, while the Jews waited in trepidation for the outcome of their fate. Eventually, he came back, stared icily at the people and, disregarding his earlier life-and-death question, demanded information about Kolya. The Besht, who knew that one could not complain to the devil that his messengers were merciless, replied that Kolya was very eager to perform his duty, and served his masters loyally. Kolya, who had been standing neglected at the side, with his henchmen in their black uniforms, did not know what was going on because he did not speak German. He was clearly as surprised as the Jews by this sudden visit and did not know what was expected of him. This was the first time that any reference to his existence had been made, and upon hearing his name mentioned, he performed a clumsy imitation of the Nazi salute, which the officer ignored. He continued to ask questions about Kolya's administration, which the Besht tried to sidestep diplomatically. Once again the officer began mocking his answers, but it became evident that the sting was directed more at Kolya's ineptness. The

officer motioned to a soldier, who turned out be an interpreter, and to Kolya, to come near, and informed Kolya that
this Jew had only wonderful things to say about him.
Without a moment's hesitation, Kolya decided to return the
compliment and offered a slew of praises in honor of the
Besht, which the interpreter relayed faithfully. The officer's
smile broadened maliciously, as the Besht tried to protest that
Kolya was too kind. He silenced them both and informed
Kolya that it was a shame that he had such high regard for
the Jew because he was about to shoot him. In fact all of them
were to be shot, and would Kolya and his men mind serving
as the firing squad. Within a few minutes, eager to please,
Kolya had more then twenty men lined up at attention, ready
to receive rifles in order to do the job. The officer informed
him that no German soldier would hand over his rifle of his
own free will: was it not possible that Kolya could produce
his own rifles? Kolya pretended to understand this fine point
of military practice and requested at least a half an hour for
his men to procure the arms.

KOLYA, THE LACKEY AND THE FOOL

This frightful exchange took place loud and clear, in German
and Ukrainian, for the express benefit of the Jewish adults
gathered. The realization, that within the space of a half an
hour their lives would come to an end, brought cries of
distress and terror. Soon the firing squad returned, with a
varied collection of firearms, ready and willing to do their
master's bidding. Kolya was in his glory, as he barked orders
to his own private army to show their stuff and impress the
German officer. The officer was not impressed, however,
because within about a minute, Kolya's army of the Free
Ukrainian State was disarmed and disbanded. Sometimes
miracles can come in pairs, because in the next instant the
order was given to release the Jews.

There were many versions and stories that revolved

around this incident, including the idea that this was the miracle of Purim for the Jews of Kortiless. As we later discovered, however – because once the order was given to release them, no Jews stayed around to find out what happened to Kolya – it was the Besht who was closest to the truth. The officer had no orders to kill. This officer and his men, although part of the murderous system which was like an evil serpent, were not the part containing the poisonous fangs, unlike the Gestapo and the SS, who did not need any special orders to terminate life at a whim. For this officer it was simply a training maneuver in the art of rounding-up and containing the civilian population for a given time, and he improvised, as the situation arose, for his own amusement. He had no interest in Kolya's administrative ability, but when all the unauthorized firearms appeared as he had requested, he confiscated them and enjoyed the process by which he had tricked the stupid man into revealing his cache. It is true that the lives of Jews were spared that time, but it was not the miracle of Purim because Haman (Kolya) remained in his position of power when the Germans departed, quickly and in an orderly manner, despite having had his feathers ruffled.

Kolya took this treatment badly, of being shown to be the lackey of his superior masters. His own cohorts accused him of stupidly betraying the Ukrainian cause by revealing the existence of the firearms. It did not take Kolya long to find a scapegoat to take the blame for his own stupidity. He arrested my Uncle Shmilke, and accused him of betraying him to the Germans by revealing to them the secret that he had earlier confided in him. No amount of ironclad proof to the contrary could convince Kolya to drop this ludicrous charge. This time the encounter ended tragically for my uncle, because Kolya sent him off, with a number of other young men, to a forced labor detail from which none of them ever returned.

EVERYBODY IS IN ON THE KILLINGS

Conditions for the Jewish community of Kortiless went from bad to worse. They began to suffer casualties, not so much at the hands of Germans in the forced labor details, but mainly at the hands of various armed marauding Ukrainian groups. Some of these called themselves Partisans, who favored Russia; others went by the name of Bulbovtsi, who were Ukrainian nationalists; and there where those who were plain criminals. These groups fought amongst themselves, and the only thing they had in common was that they robbed from farmers and killed Jews. Kolya's position became precarious and one day, for his own safety, he disappeared. His presence had not added to law and order nor contributed to anyone's security, and the Germans never bothered to appoint a new administrator.

There was one particular group of bandits who invaded Kortiless. They paraded around the village in broad daylight, abusing and beating up Jews and Gentiles alike. Having marked their victims during the day, at night they invaded their homes, dragged out a number of Jewish women and girls and raped them. Uncle Bentse, who tried to intervene on behalf of Tanya, was beaten and knocked senseless. The community was left in bitter mourning over the incident. At that time, I did not understand the severity of the situation, because as far as I knew, the only victim was my uncle and he survived. We went to cheder – this was for the last time – and the rebbe was very mellow and gentle with us. Instead of the usual lesson, he made us recite portions of the songs in unison, while he walked around us, with tears in his eyes, patting our heads. He called us 'shayne shepselach' (beautiful lambs), and told us to run straight home.

One of the girls who was raped had a brother named Chonen. He was physically one of the most powerful men of Kortiless. This physical quality must have been a great advantage to his father's business of cattle and horse-trading. Robbers were always plentiful, but not one of them ever got the upper hand on Chonen as he moved his livestock to and from the *yarid* (market). He was involved with his brothers in this trade during the Polish and Russian occupation. The Germans put an end to it, however, and Chonen, who did not trust them and particularly disliked Kolya, took to the woods and managed to survive with great ability. He tried to encourage and persuade other Jewish young men to join him but all of them refused because of family and other reasons. On the night of the rape, Chonen was not at home. He appeared several days later and swore to avenge his sister's honor like Jacob's sons who avenged the honor, of their sister, Dina. Anyone who tried to dissuade him from his mission of vengeance was scornfully rejected. He visited my Uncle Bentse, who was still convalescing from the beating, and lifted him like a baby from the bed and hugged him for his courage in trying to prevent the rape. Chonen did not evolve any elaborate plan to exact his vengeance. Within a very short time, he tracked down the bandits and requested to join them. It was no problem for him to pass as a Ukrainian. As their leader offered his hand to welcome him, Chonen pulled out a knife and stabbed him repeatedly, at the same time screaming out the reason why he was doing it. By the time he was shot he had taken three of them, including their leader, to their graves.

The bandits' reprisal came quickly and was merciless. They killed about thirty Jews, amongst them my maternal grandparents, Berchik and Fruma, my Uncle Bentse, and Tanya. They would have killed everyone that night if it were not for the fact that another group, the Partisans, happened to come by the village, and fighting broke out between them – not that they were anxious to save the Jews, but they were eager to obtain the bandits' arms.

My parents, my brother and I happened to be away that night visiting Ukrainian farmer friend. Despite the fact that we had already experienced calamity – there was no doubt that both my uncles, Shmilke and Yerachmiel, were dead – there are no words to describe the grief we felt, particularly

Mother, when we returned to discover the mutilated bodies of our loved ones. There was not a Jewish person in Kortiless who did not lose a close member of his family in this carnage. The small number that was left to mourn the dead, gathered at the cemetery, heedless of their own safety, and offered them their last rites. There was no comfort for those who were still alive because everyone knew, in their hearts, that their days were numbered.

Regardless of how difficult and hopeless the situation was, we somehow managed to find the courage to continue with our lives. My father refused to accept the fatalist concept that it was God's will whether we should live or die. On the contrary, he argued, it was God's will that we should live and we had to help Him in that wish. Mother was still in mourning and had lost all desire to live, but Father would argue with her and beg her to take heart for our sake. Many Jewish homes, which had once enjoyed the joys and hardships of life, now stood empty. The angel of death had many helpers to perform his task and almost every day we discovered new victims of his labor. The four of us moved in with my paternal grandparents because my father was concerned for their safety. He had no means by which to protect them but he felt better being close to them. 'At least we shall die together', was a common sentiment in those bitter days. As strange as it may seem, there were people who actually believed that since the situation was so bad, it could only become better. Others gave up on that hope and tried to reach another town or village. Father decided, with two other men in the village, to maintain a constant vigil so that if they heard anything they would have sufficient time to get the family out of the house and hide. One early dawn, my father heard the drone of motors coming from the north of town. That meant Germans. Within minutes, since we slept in our clothes, we were up and out of the house, taking with us only those things that we had decided upon before, which had been placed within easy reach. Next to my grandparents' house was a large cornfield, and the six of us, quickly but carefully – in order not to leave a trail of broken corn stocks, entered it as far as we could go and lay down quietly. We heard the Germans arrive and soon saw the smoke and the flames from my grandparents' house lighting up the sky. We were aware of the sounds of destruction, the cries of despair, and realized that this was the end of our life in Kortiless. At nightfall, we began our trek towards the city of Ratno.

2 Ratno: Last Temporary Refuge

In the late spring of 1942, my paternal grandparents and the four of us came to Ratno, a small city about fifty kilometers from Kortiless. So did the rest of the remaining Jews of Kortiless and those from other villages around the area. Because of various marauding groups, life in the villages, especially for Jews, was unbearable. Ratno was not exactly a haven but the local Jewish community council (*Judenrat*) made every effort to accommodate us by providing us with identity papers and shelter, and sharing with us whatever little food they possessed. We stayed with relatives. To somehow relieve the suffering of the children, at least the ones who were old enough to work, they were handed over to farmer acquaintances in the vicinity. This arrangement served a number of objectives: the children were fed, their families would occasionally receive some food from the farmer and most important of all, in the event of an *akzia* (massacre) in Ratno, their lives would be spared. My brother became a candidate for this kind of arrangement. My father knew a farmer who was willing to accept him. It was not an easy decision to send a child off into a situation like that, because even under the direst circumstances we tried to stay together, but despite my parents' reservations, the farmer came one day and took away my brother. It was the first time I had ever been separated from my brother under such circumstances. The time when he lived with my grandparents, when I was on the farm, did not have any effect on me, but this new experience of being separated from my brother added another dimension of sorrow to my lot. As it turned out, my brother did not have an easier time of it.

Those children who, in their physical appearance, blended in with their Ukrainian counterparts, managed to escape abuse and being molested by their peers, at least. My brother was a beautiful child, with dark eyes, black hair and a dark complexion. It was obvious that he was not Slavic. Consequently, he was not spared the torments and taunts of the children, and the neighbors began accusing the farmer of harboring a Jewish child. My brother's longing for his family contributed to his woes and I knew that my parents were considering bringing him back. Mother would visit him as frequently as possible and return miserable and depressed, yet it was felt that this was his best chance for survival. I always wanted to accompany my mother on her visits, and I would cry bitterly when refused. The reason given for the refusal was that it was too far for me to walk. I refused to accept and insisted that I could do it. On one particular occasion, when mother was about to set out for her visit, I once again insisted upon joining her. When I realized that my pleas of wanting to see my brother would not succeed, I threw a tantrum. Evidently it must have been impressive, because it was agreed that I could join her.

Travel restrictions were placed upon Jews. Any Jew discovered outside his restricted area paid with his life. The only way Jews traveled was by cover of darkness. My brother's place was located in a restricted area. Every time Mother went on her visits, she would take her life in her hands. To escape detection, she would set out at dusk and return way past midnight, the following day. Ratno is located in an area called the Pripet Marshes (on the Pripet River). The only entrances to the town were by two bridges, one located on each side. At night, one Ukrainian policeman was placed on each bridge to prevent Jews from leaving the town. The guards, however, did not particularly enjoy their boring task and would frequently abandon their posts, from about midnight, in favor of some more enjoyable activity, or if they did not abandon them completely, they would be fast asleep. At such times my mother would slip back into the city.

It did not require long explanations for me to grasp the danger of our journey, and that my coming along simply increased the risk of being captured. Yet for some reason – because of my tantrum, or perhaps it was divine providence – it was decided that this time I would accompany my mother. Incidentally, the reason that my father could not join us was because Jewish men had to report every morning at the police station for various work details.

At dusk, just prior to when the sentries manned their positions, we set out. It was summer and I insisted on walking barefoot, but my mother made me carry my shoes and a warm coat. My mother was like a cat: silent, agile and sure-footed. She, of course, knew the way and warned me in advance of the difficulties that lay ahead, like farmhouses that had big dogs and had to be avoided. Finally I had to put on my shoes because as I became more tired, I would drag my feet and stub my toes and cry out. In order to make up for lost time, because of my pace, my mother simply carried me on her back. Piggyback was a game I played only with my father, but this was no game. Our lives depended on reaching my brother's place before daylight. I was full of admiration for my mother's ability to nearly double the pace, with me on her back. Secure in my mother's care, I nearly began to doze off when suddenly she stopped, heaved me off her back and clamped a hand over my mouth to silence my protests. I heard the noise of approaching vehicles and saw the sky brightly lit by their headlights. The only ones who traveled in motor vehicles were Germans and here we were, completely in the open. Despite my tiredness, with the help of my mother – it must have been the fastest hundred-yard dash of my life – we literally ran for our lives away from the road. We flattened ourselves and tried to become part of the earth. We were close enough to hear the sounds of the soldiers' voices above the roar of the motors. There must have been about ten trucks filled with soldiers and a couple of smaller vehicles. To avoid ambush by partisans, they traveled a considerable distance apart. Each time we were bathed in the light of a new vehicle I was certain that this time we would be discovered. It took about a half an hour, I imagine, for the last vehicle to pass, but it seemed like an eternity. We stayed rooted to the spot, for a long time, until all the noise subsided. My mother stood up first and then she raised me and began hugging me as tears streamed down her face. I realized that there was only one reason for this convoy to be heading in the direction of Ratno, at this time of night:; it was bent on doing the devil's work, an *akzia* (massacre).

Realizing that I would never see my father again, I cried bitterly, and my mother could do very little to comfort me in my grief except hold me in her arms, rock me gently and join me in my tears. I had already experienced the excruciating pain of the loss of loved ones, and the sorrow and loneliness that such loss leaves in its wake. The knowledge that in a matter of a few hours I would lose my other grandparents and my father brought a level of pain that was beyond description. My young heart was too fragile to bear such grief and I would have gladly exchanged my life for his. All desire to continue with life was drained from our veins and in fact at one point we decided that the best thing to do would be to finish it all and return to Ratno. The only reason we did not pursue this course was out of consideration for my brother. To leave him orphaned, through our own choosing, was an unpardonable sin. There was another reason as well. My mother was a religious woman and she believed that the fact that I had been allowed to accompany her this time was a miracle – an act of God. Furthermore, she expressed faith in the Almighty and in my father's ability somehow to survive the massacre. Without haste or fear but with resignation, leaving our fate in the hands of the Almighty, we continued our course in the direction of my brother.

It was a simple matter to blockade the town of Ratno by placing a couple of Germans on the two bridges. Only those who were lucky enough to know how to swim or were familiar enough with the area to negotiate the marshes managed to escape. The river was not particularly wide and an average swimmer could easily make it, but there were some who drowned from panic and exhaustion – and the leeches: anyone who spent more than fifteen minutes in the water was simply covered with them. As for the marshes, the prospect of escape there was not much greater and it became the eternal resting-place for many of our people.

The round-up of Jews, with the help of Ukrainian police and officials, did not present a problem. All Jewish homes were marked with a yellow Magen David and the homes were thoroughly searched, the occupants rounded up and brought to a central place in the town, near the synagogue. Those who tried to escape were shot in the street. The younger and stronger men were picked first and sent to the outskirts of the town, where they began digging a communal grave. When they finished digging, to the satisfaction of the officer, they were lined up at the mouth of the grave and were the first ones to be shot. Having completed that phase, they began to load up trucks with the Jews in the square and delivered them to the execution site. To diminish the problem of handling the frightened and hysterical people, who knew what was awaiting them, they brought them to the gravesite no more than two trucks at a time. To gather the bodies of those who tried to run away or those shot in the streets of the city took more effort than shooting them, all lined up, in front of the open grave. Time was saved by not bothering to check whether those who fell into the grave were really dead because at the end they would be covered up anyway. In the event that there was a sign of life or groaning, a few more shots were fired in that direction, not as a coup de grâce but as a sport.

When my father heard the trucks, he realized that the massacre was taking place and managed to escape the house minutes before the Germans barged in. His first thought was to try and reach his parents, who lived in his late brother's house with their daughter-in-law. By the time he reached the house he saw, from his place of cover, that he was too late, for the occupants, including his father, were being led away. The reason his mother was not amongst them was because she had been summoned, late at night, to aid in the delivery of a Ukrainian child on the outskirts of town (we learned this much later). My father waited for a long time in the hope that his mother was still hiding and that he would find her and lead her to safety. Because the search was becoming more intensified and he feared that soon he would be discovered, he decided to try to make his escape across the marshes. He was accosted by a number of Ukrainians who were just waiting for this kind of prey. His begging and pleading for his life made very little impression upon them and they led him away and handed him over to the Germans.

It was late in the day and the Germans were conducting their mopping-up activity by gathering the last victims, like my father, for the final truckload. Two Germans were guarding four other men in the group to which my father was added, amongst them the man from Kortiless known as the Besht. My father turned to him and asked, 'So this is what our end will be like?' the Besht replied, 'Only the Creator of the universe knows what the end will be like.' Their conversation was interrupted by the order to lie down. Assuming that they were going to be shot down on the street, the Besht began pleading to be taken to the communal grave, but his request was cut short by a shot from one of the Germans. As the Besht yelled out in pain and fell to the ground, my father reached for the muzzle of the rifle, still pointing, and yanked it from the soldier's hands. Flailing it like a bat he managed to hit the neck of the second soldier, who was about to fire his rifle, with a forceful blow that sent that him reeling, and my father ran with all his might in the direction of the river. On the way he dropped the rifle because it was impeding his progress. The remaining three Jews used the opportunity of the God-given commotion and ran as well. My father managed to reach the river and, despite the fact that he did not know how to swim, entered the water up to his neck. He made the decision that if he was pursued, he would drown himself rather than fall into German hands. While he was standing there, feeling the slimy leeches attaching themselves to his body, he saw a Ukrainian in a rowboat approaching him. My father was suspicious of the man's intentions, but had no other alternative, and heaved himself into the boat. If the man rowed in the direction of the city, my father would try to overpower him. The man rowed my father safely to the other shore, however, and even wished him good luck. There were some good Ukrainians, even if my father, until this day, claims that this was an angel. Now that he was temporarily safe, he became aware of the leeches that stuck to him and he pried them off with disgust. Exhausted by the superhuman effort he had expended, and emotionally drained by the realization that he was all alone in this world, he fell asleep.

RACHEL'S STORY

I wish to relate the story of one of the survivors who was subjected to the long, tortuous journey from her home to the gravesite. This story I heard right after the war, from the lips of the survivor as she told it to my parents. The lady's name is Rachel. At the time of the massacre, Rachel was in her early twenties, married, and the mother of a 2-year-old child. They lived with her parents and her brother. The Germans barged into the house with barbaric force, shouting orders, upsetting and breaking everything in their way. The tactic was to stun the victims into docility by brute force. It was early in the morning and no one was dressed yet. Rachel's father was very sick and could hardly move, but a soldier stood over him shouting, '*Raus! Schnell!*' When the results of her father's efforts to get up were unsuccessful, the soldier hit him over the head with a rifle. Rachel's brother, who was in the room, tried desperately to explain that he would carry his sick father, but failed in his pleading. Seeing the blood running from his father's head, he shoved the soldier aside in an effort to come to his father's aid, but two quick shots put an end to that valiant and heroic son. In the little house, the shots sounded like thunder. The three adults were stunned beyond fear by the events that had just taken place and suffered in silence, but the child began to cry. The irritation on the face of the German, at the noise of the baby, was forbidding. Fearing the worst, Rachel forcefully put a hand over the child's mouth, while her husband wrapped them in a blanket, which he grabbed from the bed, to help smother the sound.

Only five minutes had passed from the time the Germans barged into the house until they were outside. Five minutes that destroyed a lifetime. Rachel's husband was immediately taken away, still struggling to finish dressing, while she was trying desperately to control the baby's wailing, and at the same time offering comfort to her grieving mother. Her father and brother were dead and in the arms of their Maker. They were spared the torture that lay ahead for those who were still alive and counting the minutes that brought them closer to their inevitable execution.

They waited for a long time in front of their house, as did their other Jewish neighbours, while the Germans watched them. Eventually a truck came along and once again the soldiers began shouting, shoving and beating those within their range to hasten their ascent into the truck. The truck moved along slowly, making frequent stops to pick up more cargo, and the scene of violence kept repeating itself at each stop. As far as the Germans were concerned, they were handling garbage and not human beings. When the truck was full it proceeded directly to the area of the synagogue and there they were made to jump off, quickly of course, to the amusement and laughter of their satanic torturers at seeing the clumsiness with which the elderly performed this feat. Some escaped with bruises while many of them ended up with fractured limbs. The absence of the younger and able-bodied men was conspicuous and Rachel later discovered the reason for this. Fear, hopelessness and the signs of life being drained away were evident in everyone's eyes. Some accepted their fate with quiet resignation; many cried bitterly; others stared blankly in disbelief that this was happening to them. There were those who prayed and recited psalms, and here and there, there were outbreaks of hysterics. The soldiers used blows and shots in the air, and if these did not work immediately, they silenced the hysterics by permanently silencing the obstinate offender. When the final truckload of people arrived, everyone was ordered to rise, line up and face the direction of the synagogue. Another act of abuse and humiliation was to take place, another bitter memory that the Jews of Ratno were to take to their communal grave. Only demented and demonic brains, filled with blind hatred towards their helpless victims, could carry out such skillful torture, guided by the hand of the devil.

Soldiers came out of the synagogue carrying and dragging the Torah Scrolls and dumped them, contemptuously, into one of the trucks, while another one poured some gasoline at the entrance. An officer followed holding a big Pentateuch in his hands; he opened it, tore out a number of pages and flipped it back to the entrance of the synagogue. He rolled the pages into a torch, lit it and from it lit a cigarette dangling from his mouth. He then picked out what seemed to him the most prominent Jew, handed him the torch and ordered him to set fire to the synagogue. The poor man did as he was told but instead of rushing away as the wooden structure erupted, he moved closer and stood in front of the raging fire. With a trembling voice but with amazing force he recited Shma Yisroel (Hear O Israel). The officer realized what the man was doing, pulled out his pistol and shot him, not out of mercy but to deny him his act of courage of Kiddush *Hashem* (Sanctity of God). Rachel knew and identified the man who did it. He was a timid man, who in his lifetime was not known for particular acts of courage. I always imagined that the man was my Zeide Meir, an impressive-looking, God-loving man, with a long white beard and the dignity of human courage. Although the Germans and Ukrainians laughed and shouted as the synagogue began to burn, they were soon silenced and awed by the old man's deed. As for the Jews, his act did not save their lives but they took with them to their grave, his lesson of human dignity and courage.

While the synagogue was still burning, consuming the martyr at its entrance, two trucks were being loaded up using the familiar tactics. As soon as these were full and had moved out, another two trucks were filled and waited for the order to move. Rachel, holding on to her child and still wrapped in the blanket despite the summer heat, boarded with her mother one of the last trucks. It was a short drive, to an open field on the outskirts of town. The truck pulled up close to the grave and they were told to descend and line up in front of it. A few, out of desperation, tried to run away. Those who were caught were brutally beaten and dragged back and the others, who managed to gain some distance, were simply shot, as was evidenced by the bodies scattered in the field.

Rachel, hugging her child tightly with one hand, and with the other leading her mother, lined up with about fifty people, and felt that her knees were giving way when she saw the lifeless bodies in the grave. She even managed to recognize some of the people and understood the conspicuous absence of the younger men, for they were the ones who had dug the grave and were now lying in it. Everybody was lined up, to the commanding officer's satisfaction, and the order was given to fire. The bodies began to fall into the open grave. Rachel felt dizzy, her mother's lifeless body let go of her hand, the baby gave a sudden jerk, slipped from her arm and fell into the grave, and she fell in after it.

Rachel opened her eyes, dazed, but somehow managed to compose her thoughts enough to realize that she was alive and must have fainted, for she felt no pain, except in her heart, because she was lying on the still warm but lifeless body of her child. The blanket was still partially covering her and very slowly she took long painful breaths. A body was heaved upon her and she nearly cried out in pain but bit her lip to stifle it. The rest of the bodies were collected from the field, and she noticed a truck with a special attachment, at one end of the grave, beginning to cover it Rachel became paralyzed with fear at the prospect of being buried alive. As the shovel came closer, she considered standing up so that she might be shot. Suddenly the roar of the motor stopped, because of a malfunction in the vehicle or because the shovel broke. For a while the soldiers began to cover the grave using hand shovels but their progress was slow and since it was getting dark, they were ordered to stop, a few meters from where Rachel lay holding her breath. The Germans were in no hurry to cover the corpses and returned to Ratno to do some looting of empty Jewish houses and rest from their long day of doing the devil's work. When she was certain that there was no one alive around, Rachel crawled out of the grave, wrapped in the blanket stained with her child's blood, and began another saga of survival.

REUNITED WITH MY BROTHER

At dawn, my mother and I arrived at the farm where my brother stayed. Exhausted, with heavy aching hearts and tears in our eyes, we took cover in a barn until the household arose. The delight with which I anticipated meeting my brother was overshadowed by the terrible news we bore. The tears of joy with which my brother greeted us continued to flow as they turned to sorrow, when we told him of our meeting with the convoy and our suspicion of the inevitable massacre. It did not take long to confirm our assumption, because by mid-morning, one of the farmers told our host about it. He embellished the events with additional information about how some farmers joined the carnage and finished the job for the Germans by hacking with axs those victims who managed to escape Ratno. Killing Jews was like hunting animals. It became an 'open season' on Jews the minute an official massacre took place in the vicinity, although there were plenty of poachers around all the time. Right then it was 'open season' and our host was unwilling to harbor the fox

while the baying hounds were in the vicinity and blood-
thirsty. He agreed, however, to hide us in the barn, offered us
some food and told us that by nightfall we were to leave. As
he crossed himself, he added, 'May God have mercy on you.'

It was hot and suffocating in the barn and once we had to
crawl deeply into the hay and cover ourselves because, as the
farmer suspected, some of the 'hunters' came to look for my
brother. The farmer told them that he got rid of the 'pest'
earlier, by sending him off in the direction of Ratno. Some of
them were not completely convinced and conducted a search
of the premises, including a cursory glance inside the barn.
Satisfied, they congratulated the farmer upon the original
idea of sending off an 8-year-old *Szyd* on such a suicidal
journey. Grateful to the farmer for his resourcefulness in
saving our lives, we realized that we could not possibly
depend on his hospitality any longer. In the evening my
mother went over to the farmer to thank him. He was
nervous, and anxious for us to be as far away from his
property as possible for the sake of his own safety, but he
succumbed to my mother's pleading and offered us food and
some articles of clothing. Except for avoiding the direction of
Ratno, we had no idea which way to turn. My brother remembered that there was a forest, not too far away, where the
farmer's wife took him to pick mushrooms, and we decided to
head for it, with him leading us. What seemed to my brother
as not too far with a horse and buggy in daylight became quite
far at night, as we constantly made detours to avoid
farmhouses. Somehow we did manage to reach the forest,
and having penetrated what we felt was deeply enough, we
fell to the ground from exhaustion and went to sleep. It is
amazing how concepts change due to circumstance.
Ordinarily, the idea of finding myself in a forest in the middle
of the night, with only my mother and older brother to
protect me, would have sent shivers of fright to the marrow of
my bones, but then it constituted safety.

FEAR OF DEATH DEHUMANIZES

Mother shook us awake, after what seemed like a very short sleep, but it was broad daylight. She seemed frightened and when we heard voices emanating from somewhere in the forest we also became apprehensive. When we located the direction from which they were coming, our immediate instinct was to put as much distance as possible between us and the source. Our ears, however, discerned the sound of children's voices in the din and we felt that did not pose any danger. Our curiosity got the better of us and we started walking carefully in the direction of the noise. As we came closer we even picked out words spoken in Yiddish. We therefore joined the group with full confidence and with the expectation of relief from our helplessness. There were at least twenty people in the group and we were surprised by the obvious hostility with which the three of us were greeted. There were two families with five children between them, and the rest were single. It soon became apparent that the commotion and the arguments were between the families and single people, and centered on squatter rights in the forest. The single people felt that children were a burden and a threat to their safety and wanted the families to move on, whereas the families argued that they were there first and had a perfect right to remain. It was an absurd situation into which we had walked and my mother, who was not one to be easily intimidated, held her ground. 'You have lost compassion', she told them, 'and are wasting your energy on useless arguments instead of trying to work out some plan of action whereby you can help each other.' She was, of course, the champion of the families. It became evident that my mother was asking for the impossible and no one had any concrete idea or the faintest clue of what to do. Her remarks did have a sobering effect for a while and the squabbling stopped, but it resumed as soon as some child made too much noise. My mother realized that there was not one person in the group on whom she could depend to take charge, and that by sitting around, even quietly, a group of this size would quickly be discovered and annihilated by the hostile population as soon as they began foraging for food. In the meantime she formulated her own plan and decided that our best chance for survival was not in numbers. The blind could not lead the blind, as the helpless could not help the helpless. There was no comfort in numbers: they simply constituted more victims. Without even bothering with the formalities of leave-taking, she told us to get up and follow her.

A DECISION IS MADE – WE RETURN TO KORTILESS

My brother and I were reluctant to leave the group. Despite the arguments, we felt the sensation of safety with the group as opposed to the danger that the three of us would face. Mother made the decisions, however, and we followed. When we persisted in nagging her about it and suggesting that we return, she stopped, made us sit down, untied the bag with the food and gave us each a piece of bread and a piece of onion. It was late in the day and this was our first meal. Having pacified our hunger enough to sustain us, we could listen to the voice of reason. Pointing at the bag, Mother explained that this was the source of immediate danger from the group. If they were to discover that we had some food they would force us to share it with them and we would face starvation. Food was the primary ingredient of self-preservation and when people are reduced to the state of hunted animals, they can become even fiercer in their quest for it. Amenities, which are so essential to human behavior, become meaningless when faced with survival. As I learned later, there were many casualties resulting from this struggle. Patiently, Mother explained to us that the people in the group were victims like ourselves, just as scared and helpless as we were. She showed us three small loaves of bread and some more onions and carrots and told us that, if rationed properly, they should last us for several days. In the meantime we could relieve our hunger by finding berries and mushrooms and anything else edible in the forest. Finally, she revealed to us her plan to head for Kortiless. This sounded like a good idea because the area we were in was strange territory to us and we were unfamiliar with the people and what to expect from them, although we had already learned to expect the worst, as our experiences with some of our Ukrainian neighbors in Kortiless had taught us. At least there, however, Mother knew definitely whom to avoid, and that could be a great advantage when your life is at stake. I noticed a certain amount of relief in my mother's face while she shared with us her decision to head for Kortiless instead of wandering around aimlessly. Unfortunately, relief was soon overshadowed by concern over the fact that she had no idea how to get there. We were not exactly on Main Street where we could stop the first passer-by and ask for directions. Here we were in the middle of a forest. Having entered it at night, Mother could not see its size nor the surrounding countryside, but my brother claimed that it was big. To children, all forests are big, as to the inexperienced all forests look alike. My mother's immediate concern was to avoid penetrating further into the woods, and to find some signs of civilization or some farm, and stay within its vicinity. Her plan was simple and logical. In order to reach Kortiless safely, once we learned the direction, we had to hide out in the forest during the day because of the danger from 'civilization', whereas at night we had to stick close to 'civilization' to avoid the dangers of the forest. So far, anything alive in the forest was more frightened of us than we of it: rabbits, snakes and an occasional deer. We knew there were wolves, and the ones which had tasted human flesh were particularly dangerous. There were also wild boar which when frightened could become very dangerous. Stories of farmers being mangled by wild boar, while hunting them were common knowledge. We walked for hours, searching for a way out, listening for the barking of dogs, voices or any sounds that could be identified with civilization. The only sounds we heard was the chirping of the birds, and the beating of our hearts from fear at the prospect of having to spend the night here. The sun disappeared from the tops of the trees and it was quickly becoming dark: we were resigned to the inevitable. We came across a big tree, with branches low enough for us to scale in the event of danger. After checking the area under it for ants, snakes and other crawling things, we gathered heaps of dried leaves which were to serve as mattress and blanket and decided to bed down for the night. Then we heard singing. It was the familiar chant of the farmers around Kortiless who would sing at the end of a day's work.

Without any hesitation, we abandoned the accommodation that we had so meticulously prepared, and headed for the source of the singing. The singing stopped before we reached any clearing or sign of a farmhouse, but we did manage to come across a road. That discovery was a great relief for us and we decided to follow it for a while, and suddenly we were, literally, out of the woods. By that time it was dark but we could discern a number of homes and barns spreading over a vast area, a body of water, and the fact that the forest stopped, almost in a straight line. We could not walk over, knock on a door and expect to be welcomed with open arms. It had been a long day, full of adventure and anxiety. We moved off the road, into the safety of the woods and found what seemed a comfortable place to lie down. Mother decided to be generous, because of the prospect of maybe obtaining some more food tomorrow, and gave us each a piece of bread and some carrots. Having soothed our hunger pains, and overcome by exhaustion, we went to sleep. When I opened my eyes, it was bright daylight and I sat up with a start when I realized that Mother was not around. Before I could shake my brother awake and fear had settled in, she appeared with a smile on her face, carrying big blueberries wrapped in a shirt given to us by the farmer. Except for the moment of fright, this was certainly a good way to start the day: to hear Mother say: 'Eat as much as you want, there's more where this came from.' She had been up for hours but allowed us to sleep as much as we could, although she was anxious to reconnoiter the area. When she noticed the blueberries, she kept herself busy all that time collecting them, while keeping a careful watch over us. That is how she could immediately appear when she saw me sit up in alarm.

A TRANSFORMATION TAKES PLACE

When we had consumed all the berries, Mother took the shirt they were in, shook it out and told me to remove the shirt I was wearing and put on the one with the berry stains. It was made of rough material, and although it was too big, I felt as if I was wrapped in sandpaper. The same thing was done with my pants and I removed my shoes and the dark cap. The transformation must have been startling because my mother laughed at the little *sheigetz* standing before her. It had been a long time since I attended cheder and my light-brown (almost blond) hair grew long and there was no trace of my ear locks. This masquerade may have served to disguise my physical appearance but it never altered the way I felt in my heart: Jewish. This fact of my birth I proudly bore despite the present danger it represented, and it paved my destiny in life. Maybe as a result of this experience I never went back to wearing any outward trappings of being Jewish, although I never ate a meal at my parents' home without a yarmulke (skullcap). My brother already wore the Ukrainian farmer's clothes, but on closer scrutiny, his black hair and dark complexion indicated that he was a member of the tribe of Jacob and not Esau. My mother, whom I resembled, made a few changes in her appearance as well, with a babushka on her head, a dark skirt embroidered at the hem, a rough, pale blouse, given to her by the farmer, and a colorful shawl. It was decided that from now on we would speak only Ukrainian amongst ourselves. Now we were ready to take a closer look at the settlement we had seen last night.

Carefully we walked to the edge of the forest, and from a

position of safety and cover we concluded that this was not a village but a community consisting of one or two clans. Despite our camouflage, we were not about to test its authenticity by simply walking into the settlement. We spent the whole day observing the activity of the people and becoming familiar with the lay of the land. Of particular interest to us were some of the crops that we recognized: carrots, cucumbers, radishes and others that may be eaten raw. Some of the men were digging a big hole for storing potatoes, to keep them from freezing in the winter. This was an age-old storage system based on the principle that after a certain depth the temperature of the earth is constant. The potatoes were covered with straw and a layer of earth and when finally the snow came, it served as an additional insulator. We made mental notes of the location of various edible crops and looked forward to restocking our dwindling food supply. Tomorrow we would obtain directions and head for Kortiless. It was comforting to notice that there were no dogs within sight or hearing. Mother commented bitterly on the fact that it was Friday and that we would be working on Shabbes. We were tempted to join this pastoral scene and feel the benefit of comparative freedom; maybe we would satisfy our craving for a warm meal, and most of all take shelter from what seemed like approaching rain. Mother was firm that first we had to gather food and that meant that we could not reveal ourselves until tomorrow.

SABBATH AND THE SOBBOTNIKY

As planned, at night, when we were certain that everyone was asleep, we walked into the fields and gathered up as many of the vegetables as we could carry back to the safety of the woods. We ate our Friday night meal of bread, cucumbers and radishes and for dessert some more blueberries. Miraculously, the threatening clouds and thunder disappeared and the rain did not come. The gnawing fact that this was the first Friday night without Father reopened the wounds of sorrow and we lay on the ground sobbing bitter tears, until we finally fell asleep. In the morning we took our cache of food, hid it safely, marked the spot and set out for the settlement. When we reached the outskirts of the forest, it was a complete surprise to us to find no one working in the fields. We saw people moving about dressed for a festive occasion in what constituted their finery: embroidered shirts and blouses, the younger women with colored ribbons in their hair and embroidered aprons. Mother realized the significance of the festive mood and explained that these people were known as Sobbotniky. They were Christians in all respects except that they believed in the sanctity of the Sabbath instead of Sunday. According to Mother, these people were in many ways discriminated against because of their supposedly eccentric and peculiar deviation: consequently they were gentler and more tolerant of Jews. We could not possibly ask for a luckier break and therefore we walked over to the closest house and greeted the people.

There was some confusion at first and many questions, and judging from their excitement, it was a rare occurrence for strangers to walk into their midst. They were getting ready to conduct their prayers and we were cordially invited to join them. Mother decided to reveal the truth to these people, that we were Jewish and that we had survived the massacre that had taken place in Ratno a few days ago. They, of course, expressed their sympathy and insisted that we join them in their services. We were assigned to the care of a family. The head of the family was a big, robust, no-nonsense man; who demanded and received immediate obedience, as we soon learned, from his own brood and his wife. There were no arguments with this man, a well-aimed glare was sufficient for everyone to do his will. We were taken to the barn by one of his sons and shown a place where we could stay, and soon the man and his wife came to ask us to accompany them to the service, attended by the community. There was really no way to decline this invitation without dire results to our safety, and with a nod from Mother we took part in the goyish

67

service, conducted by our host. These people did not care who you were as long as you behaved like them and did what they did. So much for tolerance. The incongruity of the situation – of having to cross myself every time I was nudged by my neighbor, one of the man's sons, who was initiating me in the rites – is difficult for me to describe. The irony of the 'Sabbath meal', which followed the services, consisting of *chazir* (pig's meat) and preceded by a long grace, while we bowed our heads in silence, has stayed with me for the rest of my life. I will never forget the sensation of filling my belly and emptying my soul.

SECURITY AND THE JEWISH QUESTION

After we had eaten our fill for the first time in many months – because essentially, since the German invasion, food, especially for Jews, had become a scarce commodity – the three of us went over to the pond to wash up. I was surprised to hear Mother speak to us suddenly in Yiddish, and the content was even more surprising. . She told us that we must leave this place as soon as possible. To my brother and me it sounded like a decision to abandon security and face the uncertainty and dangers outside, so obviously we wished to know the reason. Mother's answer was phrased in a question: 'Do you wish to remain Jewish?' No doubt she knew the answer, and we were not even aware of the connection between this question and the issue at hand, but we added our confirmation with sincerity and conviction. Mother explained that these people would offer us sanctuary but not as Jews, and if we continued to receive their hospitality for an extended period, we would be obliged to become part of their community. My brother protested that we could withstand the pressure, offering as proof the fact that his stay with the farmer had had no effect on him. It was one thing to send away a child to improve his lot and maybe even save his life, but the inevitability of our becoming Sobbotniks in front of her eyes was too much for my mother to bear. We had to accept her decision despite the danger that was lurking in our path the minute we left this place and the fact that our chances of our avoiding it were almost non-existent.

We enjoyed their hospitality for a few more days – exactly how many I do not remember – during which time Mother's suspicions of their intentions were verified. These people belonged to a sect, and consequently they were zealous in their beliefs and particularly mindful of their potential converts, namely my brother and me. After doing our share of the chores in the field and around the house, we received a daily portion of indoctrination into Christianity, with a degree of dogmatism which made the cheder, by comparison, look like the English parliament. Mother tried several times to broach the subject of our departure by first thanking them, profusely, for their hospitality and kindness. She even embellished the story with the fact that her husband was waiting for us in Kortiless, and said she would be grateful to them if they could give us directions. To our dismay, the man claimed that he did not know exactly how to get there but there was a big village not too far away, where the information could be obtained in a couple of days. In his opinion it was foolish to endanger all our lives on such a journey and his best suggestion was for Mother to leave the two of us behind in his care, while she went alone to Kortiless and brought back our father. We were dumbstruck when Mother eagerly agreed to this plan, since we assumed that Father was dead. We were confused by Mother's consent and luckily we did not contradict her, but genuinely began to cry and object to this plan. Mother tried to comfort us by telling us that it was a very good idea for her to go alone and that she would come back for us very soon, with our father. The threatening glare on the man's face indicated to us that we had had our say and had best be quiet while our elders were talking. Mother asked for – and received – a generous amount of provisions for her journey and told the man that she would leave early in the morning, then dragged us, still whimpering, to the barn where we slept.

Upon entering the barn, Mother told us softly in Yiddish that we should once again set up a wail, and then she scolded us loudly in Ukrainian: 'Stop your crying! These nice people are giving us good advice. It will be much easier for me to look for Father on my own. In the meantime you will be safe here until I return with Father.' Satisfied that this last exchange would be heard properly by our hosts, she then held us tightly in her arms and told us that she would never leave us behind in this place. Mother explained that had she insisted upon taking us with her, her life would have been in danger. These people were determined to 'save our souls', and therefore Mother had to be as convincing as possible in her pretense that she was going alone. When we were certain that everyone was asleep, we gathered our few belongings, shared the precious food amongst ourselves and quietly sneaked away into the night, without the slightest knowledge in which direction to run.

MY FATHER IS ALIVE BUT NOT WELL

Father awakened from his weary and troubled sleep to discover that he had lost his memory. The only way his mind could cope with the physical effort and mental strain which he had undergone only hours ago, was to deny that this was happening to him. The realization that he was alone in the world triggered a kind of temporary amnesia, denying him his past. Eventually he began to experience intermittent flashes of memory that made him aware that his life was in grave danger and that he must avoid contact with any human being. It was getting dark and that offered him a sense of security, but he had the sensation that he was very hungry. Under cover of darkness he began to walk aimlessly in search of food, which he finally found many hours later in a farm field. Having abated his hunger with raw vegetables, he continued his march without any destination in mind. Dawn was beginning to break and with it the awareness that he was exposed to danger. He sneaked into a barn, burrowed into the hay and went to sleep.

Some hours later, dogs picked up the scent of my father in the barn, and their persistent barking woke him from his deep sleep. Realizing the dire predicament he was in, he armed himself with a rake. Eventually the farmer became aware of the dogs' incessant barking and came over to investigate. He opened the barn door and one of the big dogs excitedly ran in after his prey and was received by my father with an enthusiastic swat with the rake. By this time more of the farmer's family were attracted by the commotion and came over in time to see their big dog come scurrying out of the barn yelping in pain. They went inside to investigate the cause of it and discovered my father standing with the rake in hand. Upon seeing the bewildered and angry faces of the farmer and his sons, Father threw away the rake and went down on his knees and began to plead, sobbingly, for his life. He must have been a sorry sight for they simply drew back and crossed themselves. Anyone who confronted him was moved to pity and even those who would, under ordinary circumstances, readily kill a Jew were reluctant to do so. It seems that this kind of reluctance, to harm the mentally unbalanced, is inherent in all cultures. I must exclude the Nazis from this kind of human behavior, however, for they eliminated even the German mentally unstable. The farmer began to interrogate my father but since he could not supply him with any answers that made sense, merely shrugging his shoulders and whimpering, the farmer decided that Father was crazy. They got him half a loaf of bread and told him to get off their property. Upon hearing the welcome news, he kissed their hands and broke into a run as fast as his feet would carry him, while the dogs chased him to the amusement of their masters.

After gaining some distance from the farm and finding that the dogs were not chasing him anymore, Father, drained of his last ounce of strength, finally stopped running. The encounter with the farmer and his dogs had given him a terrible fright and added to his confusion. He noticed a big haystack in a field and took cover inside while he recovered his strength by demolishing the half a loaf of bread. Frightened, physically and mentally exhausted, his mind and behavior reverted to a childish period; he started to cry and to express the desire to go home, but he had no idea where home was. It was in this state that he began to have memory flashes or dreams of his childhood, and the picture that was crystallizing in his mind was Kortiless. The name stayed with him and it became his destination. The fact that my mother, brother and I were not in Ratno on the day of the massacre and the possibility that we were still alive had been erased from his mind, and never dawned on him until much later. Despite his ordeal, he was in good physical condition and with the instinct of a homing pigeon he began making his way towards Kortiless.

LEIBA IS A GOOD JEW

'Leiba *dobri Szyd*' (Leiba is a good Jew). That was the consensus amongst most Ukrainians who knew my father. This reputation preceded him for many reasons. While still a young boy, during the First World War, he had served as an interpreter for the Germans. One of his functions was to accompany Germans when they went around the farms collecting livestock and other commodities to feed the army. Being blessed with a beautiful voice, my father would make up lyrics that included the items that the Germans were looking for, and sing as loudly as he could. The Germans were delighted with this impromptu concert and would encourage him to sing more, while in the meantime, the farmers would hide whatever they could. The farmers always proudly remembered this act of courage and consideration by the little Jewish boy. Later, in his adult years, he managed a farm, was familiar with livestock, and could ride a horse bareback and use a plow. In his trading and relations with other farmers he was always fair and honest and never went back on his word.

He spoke Ukrainian fluently with the proper intonations and folksy expressions; he had a gift for telling stories and a great repertoire of Ukrainian songs that delighted his listeners. Furthermore, he enjoyed the additional advantage of knowing how to read and write: a rarity amongst the Ukrainians in our area. Socially he mixed well with them and could drink any one of them under the table: again, a rare quality amongst Jews and greatly appreciated by Ukrainians. Aside from these social commitments, the only drink my father enjoyed was the kiddush (blessing) wine. Physically, my father was a strong man and although a gentle person, he would not decline a contest of arm-wrestling or other tests of strength in which he would invariably come out the winner. Above all, my father remained a proud, religious and God-loving Jew. The Ukrainians knew that and respected him for it, despite the fact that they would sometimes openly state that it was 'a shame and a waste for such a good man to remain a Jew.' This was meant, of course, to be a great compliment to Father.

Another reason for my father's popularity was the fact that he was Mareida's son. My grandmother was the closest thing to a doctor that the entire area could claim. I do not know where she gained her medical expertise. She was not born in Kortiless but came from some western country. Her maiden name was Rothschild. I have no recollection of my grandparents' home resembling a clinic, nor of any of the paraphernalia associated with medicine, except for a big, black bag which I was always curious to investigate but was never allowed to touch. In one of the rooms there was a loom which my grandfather operated and there were also bookshelves with many books in a foreign language. I loved browsing through them because they contained drawings of the human figure, and animals and their innards, while others depicted plants and strange creations. These books belonged to my grandmother. Evidently she was successful and greatly appreciated in her practice because many people owed their lives to her and remained grateful.

In his present condition, my father was unaware of his popularity amongst the Ukrainians in the vicinity of Kortiless, but some instinct continued to drive him in that direction. I must point out, however, that popularity amongst some of the Ukrainians had limited longevity, as we had sadly discovered when the Germans invaded. The details of Father's progress towards Kortiless are hazy, for obvious reasons, but within a few days he began to recognize familiar terrain. Luckily – or as my father attributed it, to divine providence – the first farmer who accosted him in the vicinity of Kortiless was a man who recognized and liked him, although my father did not remember the farmer and instinctively began pleading for his life. It took the farmer some time to convince my father that he meant him no harm and that he was free to go on his way if he so desired. The farmer was moved by the pitiful condition of my father and kept repeating his name in an effort to allay his fears, but my father's persistent whimpering and begging for his life convinced him that my father was crazy. He reluctantly left him and went in the direction of his home. Somehow the message penetrated, and like a wary and cautious dog, my father began to follow him at a safe distance. For a long time he waited near the house until finally the farmer's wife came out and left some food for him. No amount of verbal persuasion could have produced better results than this simple act. Father was ravenous but instead of attacking the food he realized, for the first time, that he must wash his hands and recite a blessing before eating. He drew some water from the well and washed his hands and face, and then he discovered that he was without a hat, which he had lost somewhere. He took off his jacket, wiped his hands and face, covered his head with the jacket, recited the blessing and then tore into the food. This instinctive act of reciting the blessing struck a familiar chord and produced a rush of memory flashes. Nevertheless, it still left him confused, and tears of stress and anxiety filled his eyes.

He knew that he had to express his gratitude for the food. Although he was still frightened of people, he gently rapped on the door and entered the house. With his jacket still covering his head, he went down on his knees, grabbed the woman's hands, kissed them and sobbed his thanks. Her heart filled with compassion at the pitiful sight of my father, whom she knew well, and she too began to cry while uttering my father's name: 'Poor Leiba. Poor Leiba.' Upon hearing his name mentioned again and again and seeing the friendly face of the woman, my father asked her, how was it that she knew him? Surprised by the question and scared by his strange behavior, the woman ran out of the house and called for her husband. Assuming that he had done something wrong and that he was in danger, my father fled the house and began to run away. The farmer chased my father, calling him by his name and yelling after him to stop, assuring him that he meant him no harm. Tired of running and overcome by the friendly pleading voice, my father stopped, turned around, looked at the approaching figure of the farmer and suddenly everything became blurred as he passed out.

TERROR FROM MAN AND BEAST

In addition to the Germans and the Ukrainians we now added the Sobbotniks to the list of our pursuers. Mother decided that the safest course, in the event that the Sobbotniks decided to pursue us, was to take the route that was definitely not bound for Kortiless but backtracked in the direction of Ratno. The primary objective, at this moment, was to gain maximum distance from the Sobbotniks during the night hours still available to us. Once again, night and the forest were our friends and protectors. We were very careful to keep to the path, which at times became narrow and indiscernible in the dark, and we continued our flight without slackening our pace until dawn.

Dawn in the forest on a summer day can be an exhilarating experience. As soon as the first rays of light begin to turn the sky gray and the morning mist becomes discernable, it is hailed by a well-rehearsed ritual of the chirping of birds. Like a virtuoso choir warming up their vocal chords, the ritual begins with the soloists and prima donnas. They have their turn at exhibiting their artistry with trills and their particular skills and eventually are joined by the rest of the company. It is a concert unparalleled by anything in its beauty and enthusiasm, and the human voice, by comparison, can at best be described as a poor imitation. By the time the sun rises, the troupe work is disbanded and then every bird continues at its own leisure. Unfortunately, we were not an enthusiastic audience nor in the frame of mind to appreciate all that beauty. My relationship with the birds, in fact, in the ensuing years that we spent in the forest, was based on a constant state of jealousy of their freedom. I begrudged them their freedom when they chirped happily in the warm days of spring and summer. My heart filled with envy when the cold days of fall approached and their singing subsided, knowing that they had migrated to a warm climate while I was left behind to face the danger of a harsh winter. The deathly silence of winter in the forest is a frightening and devastating experience.

When the sun rose we were still in the forest but we decided to leave the path and find a spot for a long overdue rest. As we lay down, we became aware of an ominous sound, which seemed not too far away, superseding in discord the symphony of the birds. It was the growling and yelping of animals, which in spite of our exhaustion made it impossible to relax. The growling became more vicious, and oblivious to the danger we inched towards the sound to investigate its cause. The view that greeted us was one of the most frightening experiences of my life. It froze the marrow of my bones and was the cause of many of my nightmares that were to follow. There were at least a dozen wolves and their cubs engaged in the process of devouring the remains of a number of human corpses. The wolves dragged and pulled at the lifeless bodies, tearing away the bloodstained garments, vying for morsels and snarling at each other. They revealed their fangs dripping with blood. The cubs licked the bloodstained ground and picked up pieces of human flesh. We may have observed this nauseating scene for no more than a few seconds, but it remained impressed on my mind for the rest of my life. Carefully and silently we retreated to the path. Overwhelmed by the danger that surrounded us on all sides, frightened and exhausted, but with superhuman effort, we tried to put as much distance as possible between us and the scene of hell we had just witnessed.

GULLIBLE PEOPLE HAVE THEIR PURPOSE

So intent were we on our flight that we did not hear the sound of a horse and wagon which approached us. The old man driving the wagon was as surprised as we were, discovering us running on the path as he came around the curve, and it was thanks to our mother's agility that she managed to pull us aside and prevent our being trampled by the horse. The man stopped and greeted us with some well-chosen curses which would have made a sailor blush, while at the same time he threateningly waved his whip at us. His bluster did not particularly frighten us, because from the trouble he had negotiating his descent from the wagon, it was obvious that he hardly presented a threat to anyone but himself. I could not contain myself and yelled out: '*Volki!*' (wolves). The man turned pale and looked around in fear, to see where they were. It was mother who filled him in on the details of what we had just observed. The old man reacted to my mother's account with a great guffaw in appreciation of the wolves' efforts to clear the forest of Jewish cadavers, which made it smell. He then told us that a few days ago, his countrymen had hunted down a bunch of Jews who were hiding in this forest, because they were stealing food from their fields, and they had decided to take them to the Germans. Those who resisted were killed on the spot. Disdainfully he described the Jews' inexperience at the task of stealing, saying that they had left a distinct trail back to their site, and that it was therefore their own fault they were caught. It did not require much deduction to realize that these were the people we had encountered previously, and that Mother's prediction of their fate was accurate.

At this point the man became curious about us, and of course his first question was: 'Are you not also dirty Jews?' Mother crossed herself and we followed suit, having gained experience in this art for the past few days, and then she abused him accordingly for having dared to hurl such an insult at us. She asked him if he was a Sobbotnik. It now became his turn to cross himself, spit and curse and vehemently deny such an ungodly accusation. We were even, and that provided the appropriate atmosphere in which to continue the conversation. Mother took charge and began to relate a tale of woe that enthralled the old man and probably stayed with him for the remaining few years of his life. She told him that we were Sobbotniks, at which point the old man again began his rigmarole of crossing himself, cursing and spitting. He was greatly relieved when Mother revealed to him that we had discovered the error of our ways and had escaped so that we could be free to practice the true religion. Offering other details – real and imaginary – of our disen-chantment with the ways of the Sobbotniks, based on our short sojourn with them, she concluded with the fact that her husband had made his escape earlier. Our objective was to reach the village of Kortiless, where he was waiting for us. The man was very sympathetic and informed us what we already knew: namely, that we were going in the direction of Ratno and that to the best of his knowledge, Kortiless was in the direction from which we had come. Mother explained to him that it was impossible for us to go there, for fear that the Sobbotniks might be looking for us, and besides, there was the danger of bloodthirsty wolves roaming this part of the forest. The man thought this over and decided that discretion was the better part of valor, and whatever pressing business he had could wait for another day, when the wolves were not frenzied by the taste of human flesh. He told us to mount the wagon and hastily turned it around, informing us that he was going to perform a good deed for our cause, from the kindness of his heart, and bring us to his village.

To deceive a gullible old man with our story was a relatively easy task but to be subjected to the scrutiny of the villagers was a different matter. It would not take long before our true identity was discovered and the three of us were added to the list of victims that these farmers already had to their credit. Mother realized the danger and began by thanking the man profusely for his generosity, adding lavishly that on the day of reckoning, this act would, entitle him to a place amongst the saints. In the same breath she begged him to give up the idea of taking us to the village, because the location of our whereabouts would be relayed to the Sobbotniks and that would place us once again in grave danger. The man became upset with Mother's intimation that anyone in the village would betray us, and pursued the point by declaring that his people were good souls and God-fearing Christians. Mother quickly agreed with the man and referred to his kindness as evidence that he must come from a village of virtual saints. Someone might inadvertently blabber, however, and the news would get back to the Sobbotniks: then not only would our souls be lost, but his efforts to save them would not count. If he took us to a desolate place, however, past the village, and pointed us to an alternate route in the direction of Kortiless, his job would be complete and consequently his reward assured. The man was silent for a minute; suddenly he spat, cursed, '*Chort vazmee*' (the devil take it), and whipped his horse into a gallop. Shortly we reached the village and when he did not slow down, Mother thanked him for his wisdom and kindness. In response, he prodded his horse to greater speed as our bones rattled. We soon passed the familiar farm where my brother stayed and had a few moments of fear of being recognized, as we tried to make ourselves invisible by lying close to the floor of the wagon. After a considerable time we reached a fork in the road, where the man stopped without warning and told us that this was as far as he was taking us. He added that we were wrong not to enjoy his hospitality. Mother gave him his due by showering him with compliments, which made the old man glow with pride, and she promised to return with her husband to visit him someday.

The road was familiar to Mother from her visits to my brother and of course we avoided the one leading to Ratno. We were exhausted from our long ordeal and were anxious to find a place for an overdue rest. But the old man left us in the open country, and although we were grateful for his help, we were also glad to be rid of him so that we could stop the pretense and revert to our own identities. His gloating over the fate of the poor Jews, massacred and handed over to the Germans by his 'good souls and God-fearing' villagers did not exactly endear him to us. Once again we were alone and too conspicuous in the open country, and our eyes were scanning the horizon for a place to hide. We noticed the outline of trees, at what seemed a great distance, and at the same time we saw some haystacks in a field not too far away. Weak from hunger and exhaustion, we headed for the heaven-sent haystacks. There were four of them close to each other and as soon as we reached them, Mother fed us. Although I was longing to sleep, I had to ask Mother why she had made references to Father, several times, as if he was still alive, knowing full well that he must have been killed in the massacre in Ratno.

THE DEAD BRING A MESSAGE FOR THE LIVING

'I had a dream', Mother replied. Patiently, savoring every word and answering our questions, she related to us the contents of her dream, which she had on the first night of our stay with the Sobbotniks. The locale of her dream was a family gathering at which there seemed to be much rejoicing, yet she knew that all the participants had been killed. Mother refused to take part in the festivities and sat dejectedly at the side. My maternal grandmother approached her and inquired why she was so sad. Mother became annoyed at the question and replied bitterly, 'How can I be happy when my Mordechai Leib is not here?' To which my grandmother responded with a hug and a happy smile: 'Of course he is not here, because he is alive.' Even if in later years this dream accumulated additional details, the basic message was the same; the dead informed my mother, that my father was alive. It was not the content of the dream that affected me so much – because dreams at that age, dreams were still too abstract a concept to understand – but to see my mother smile, to hear the excitement in her voice and joy at relating it, made me delirious with happiness. The three of us hugged each other and shed tears of joy. Within a few minutes, bolstered by one of the primary human emotions – hope – we were fast asleep.

FATHER REGAINS HIS MEMORY

Father was in a stupor for several days and was cared for by the kind couple. From time to time he would awaken and would be given something to drink or to eat. He would mumble his gratitude and cry bitterly until he passed out again. We never learned the medical reason for this phenomenon, but one of the explanations offered was that this was his way of escaping the reality of his grief. One day he opened his eyes and there was no one beside him. He got up, put on his clothes – which had been washed – and went outside. He found the couple working in their field, and after greeting and thanking them for their care, he silently joined them in their chores. At the end of the day he went back with them to the house and joined them for their evening meal. When he declined to eat the meat and realized the reason he was doing so, he quickly explained to his hosts that he was Jewish. They laughed at this superfluous information and told him that of course they knew that. At this point Father began to relate his escape from Ratno, and explained that he did not remember anything about himself, except that from time to time he had these memory flashes which haunted him. Patiently, they began to fill in gaps in his memory about his personal history, with which they were familiar. Although the entire picture of his identity was not clear in his mind, he believed the information that the good people told him about himself. When they finished, he thanked them with all the accepted graces and expressions and informed them that he was moving on to Kortiless. They warned him that it was not advisable in his condition to make that journey; furthermore, most of the village had been burned down, many of the villagers killed and those who remained primarily blamed the Jews for their misfortune. If he were to run into any one of them they would certainly try to kill him. His desire to visit Kortiless, however, superseded any consideration for his personal safety. The farmer offered him a cap and a small blanket, which he gratefully accepted, and he took his leave. Within several hours, in the middle of the night, he was standing over the ashes that were once our home, and crying. As his tears flowed, they flooded his mind with the contents and details which once comprised his life. He sat down in the middle of the rubble and allowed the full awareness of his misfortune to penetrate his mind. Although he realized that the three of us were not present in Ratno on the day of the massacre, he assumed that we were dead by now because there was no chance of our surviving, alone, the hostility of the Ukrainians. It would be useless, therefore, for him to go back to the vicinity of Ratno to search for us. Eventually he stood up and decided to investigate the rest of the village, despite the danger. Each familiar site, which was now in ruins, brought additional stabs of pain. It was nearly dawn when he reached the site of what was once his parents' home, at the other end of town. He was absorbed in his thoughts, remembering the horrible scene when our 'good neighbors' were looting and finally setting the house on fire while we were hiding in the cornfield, when someone called out to him. He turned around to discover a familiar face: a fellow nicknamed Shestak because he had a sixth digit on one of his hands. Without warning, the man attacked him, knocking my father to the ground with a powerful blow. Although he was dazed, he realized that he was fighting for his life. His hands felt the remnants of a board that must have been part of the house but had not been completely consumed in the blaze. As the man reached down, to press his advantage and grab him by the throat, my father swung the board, with all the force he could muster from the position in which he was lying, and landed it on the man's head. The man collapsed with a groan on top of my father. Father rolled him off, without investigating the extent of the damage that he had caused to the man – for in the frame of mind he was in, he would have killed him if it had been necessary – and as the first light of dawn appeared, he once again ran away from Kortiless.

AN 'ANGEL' SAVES FATHER

Now that the full awareness of his predicament had returned and the torture of his grief beset him, his fear of death had left him, but he was still governed by some sense of survival. He began to wander from one Ukrainian farmer acquaintance to another. Some of them welcomed him; others offered their sympathy but because of fear for their own safety turned him away; and many were openly hostile and abused him with threats. He finally reached a point when he realized the futility of his existence and decided that the best thing for him was to end his life by turning himself over to the Germans. The reason for this course was to save himself the humiliation that his Ukrainian captors would have heaped upon him before they disposed of him or turned him over to the Germans. He had no means by which to commit suicide, and besides, that was a sin against God. He was sorry that he had thrown away the rifle, wrenched from the German soldier's hands in Ratno. One day, when he was determined that he could not continue anymore, he decided to follow a route that would lead him to the Germans. With complete disregard for his safety he was sitting in the middle of the road, eating what he thought would be his last meal – a few pieces of stale bread – when he was approached by a man inquiring what he was doing. Father poured out his heart to the man and revealed his intention. The man was a kind of forest ranger, but whenever my father told this story, he described the man with such details as to attribute to him the aura of an angel. When he had finished listening to my father's woes and his intentions, the man became annoyed and sternly advised him against this course. He urged him to continue his struggle and said that no man had the right to throw away a gift from God; only a fool would choose an option like that. Subdued by the man's argument, and definitely convinced that the man was an angel when he miraculously took out from his pouch half a loaf of bread and gave it to my father, he changed his course and continued his struggle of survival.

MY CONFRONTATION WITH GOD

We awoke to the familiar melody of the farmers' song in the distance, signaling the end of their day's labor, and we realized that we had slept the whole day. As we looked at the setting sun, Mother suddenly squealed with delight and informed us, while pointing at the sun, that this was the general direction of Kortiless. Now that she was certain of the location of Ratno and knew that it lay east of Kortiless, it was a simple deduction, but the actual road that was to take us there was another matter. For the rest of our grueling journey, however, the setting sun guided our path. The long sleep made us hungry, and before we set out on our journey for the night, Mother doled out meager portions of our dwindling food. The food, Mother's dream and her discovery of the general direction of Kortiless combined to offer us confidence, and we anxiously began our march. It became dark quickly, as the sky was covered by black threatening clouds and the sound of thunder rumbled deeply, interspersed with occasional lightning. It was a new kind of fear which beset my young heart, as the sound of the thunder drew nearer, like the mighty wheels of a chariot racing across the sky, striking the cobblestone clouds and producing sparks of lightning. Like all children, I was always afraid of thunder and lightning but this was the first time I was completely exposed to its mercy. Silently I began to pray and reason with the Almighty. It was evident that my silent prayers were not effective, because the gathering force of the storm was increasing. I was not so much afraid of something happening to me, but the possibility of harm to my brother or my mother was an unbearable thought. To be orphaned by the forces of nature, which God controlled, was too evil a punishment for sins that I had not perpetrated and I felt I did not deserve it. I became indignant and more daring in pleading my case. I assured God that I loved Him and did not hold Him responsible for the death of my father, members of my family and my friends, because black-hearted beasts over whom He had no control caused their deaths. To subject us at this point, however, to the hazards of the elements, over which he does have control, was not only unfair, but He was venting His wrath on the helpless instead of directing it against His enemies. It began to rain and as the thunder became louder, I cried out, loudly, my taunts at God. Mother heard me screaming and asked me what I was saying. When I repeated to her that 'God was unfair! God was merciless! God was a coward!', she slapped me, not in outrage at my blasphemy but to bring me back to my senses. I cried bitterly and she hugged and comforted me and encouraged my tears to flow. As we stood huddled, there was a long streak of lightning and we noticed the outline of houses, and realised that we were in the middle of some community. How wonderful it would have been to knock on one of the doors and be invited into the safety of the house, to warm our bones and dry our clothes. Mother did not even consider that option but made us follow her hastily away from the houses.

We were now in the middle of the storm, and the rain, wind and frightful bursts of lightning followed by thunder impeded our progress. Yet we continued our march, despite our exhaustion, because there was no place for us to hide. It must have been hours later that we suddenly realized that we were walking on a bridge. We mustered all the reserves of our strength and with all haste crossed the bridge and descended below it. It was not exactly rainproof but it was a Godsend, and after we had located what seemed a relatively dry spot, we huddled together. Despite our drenched clothes and shivering bodies we did manage to fall asleep, as the storm above us raged on.

LIKE A CAGED AND DESPISED ANIMAL
THAT IS TO BE SLAUGHTERED

It was a man in a rowboat who noticed us sleeping under the bridge. Without even bothering to verify the fact, he set up a wail: *'Szydi! Szydi!'*, and within minutes there was a group of men and women surrounding us and staring at us in disgust, as if we were some cockroaches who had invaded a royal banquet. Mother tried in vain to protest, and began the tested story that we were Sobbotniks, but even before she could develop the plot, the proof of her lies was revealed to all. My brother and I were standing with our pants pulled down. A roar of laughter and ridicule went up at the indisputable evidence of our Judaism. To inflict humiliation, they prevented us from lifting our pants to cover our private parts, while they shoved, dragged and pushed us to one of the nearby houses, which we never noticed in the storm. Despite the terrible beating, taunting and shoving we received until we reached the house, none of us cried out or begged for our lives, because it was useless to expect mercy from these animals and since death was inevitable, our only hope was that it would be over quickly. We were thrown into some kind of shed and the door was barred. The only light that penetrated was through the cracks in the wall. I first felt the pain around my mouth and tasted the saltiness of my blood and realized that I must have bitten into my lips to prevent myself from crying out, and then felt the aching bruises on the rest of my body. Maybe the most humiliating and painful aspect of this experience was to watch helplessly, as my loved ones were being tortured. I cried as I observed, in the meager light, the miserable state of my mother and brother, and they joined me, crying silently, until finally our tears ran dry. We were a great novelty, so during the first hours of our internment there was a constant gathering around the shack accompanied by horrible insults, derisive jeering (Christ-killers was the favorite chant) and stone-throwing at the shack, as if it contained dangerous animals. It was finally silent outside and we tried to look through the cracks in the wall to see what was going on. We could not see anyone but we knew that our fate was being decided. The food that we had with us was taken away and now, after many hours in this dungeon, the pangs of hunger were playing havoc with our stomachs. Mother tried to comfort us with praise of our bravery, telling us that we should not lose hope and should retain our trust in God. Furthermore, if we were destined to die at the hands of these people, they would have killed us a long time ago. I took exception to the part about retaining our trust in God, and argued that He was as helpless as we were against these godless people: He could not help us. Mother tried to shush me but in the end permitted me to vent my anger until I somehow realized that I was not making sense anymore but emitting all kinds of noises. I had a fever and I was delirious. Mother held me tightly in her arms and rocked me gently, patting me and wiping the caked blood from my face. Despite my hungry, rumbling stomach and my body that was burning up, mercifully I fell asleep.

I spent the whole night in a semi-conscious state, balancing between life and death. I was aware that my mother and brother seemed to be busy with me the whole night, talking to me, massaging and patting me and constantly calling out my name while trying to elicit a response from me. I was in a haze and very weak but felt no pain and all I wanted to do was sleep. Occasionally I would hear my mother banging on the door and begging for somebody to come, but there was no response. She would return, take me in her arms, rock me gently and cry. I felt her tears dripping down onto my face and I would open my eyes for a few moments and assure her that I was fine. Somehow I managed to survive the night, but in my condition the lack of food was critical and I was beginning to fade. In my delirium I began to hallucinate, and described my visions with great effort to my mother and brother. It was peaceful and painless as I began to lose contact with this world. I told them that the clouds, on which I was lying, had sharp points, but they should not worry because it really did not bother me and that I was not afraid. Mother realized that I was dying and once again she banged on the door, trying to summon help. She saw through one of the cracks a woman, who must have heard her, continuing with her chores without even glancing in our direction. Mother's next step will always remain a mystery to me, but of course she always claimed that it was divine inspiration. She began to sing, at the top of her lungs, a famous Ukrainian folk song. Within minutes the door opened and the woman, who was previously deaf to my mother's pleading, stood there looking bewildered. Mother continue her singing as she went over and kneeled beside me. The curiosity of the woman got the better of her and she came over to my mother and asked her why she was singing. Mother explained that I was dying and this was the way she chose to make her farewell. One look at me and the woman was convinced that my mother was telling the truth, at least the part about my dying. There must have been a spark of human decency left in the woman because she ran out, not even bothering to bolt the door, and within minutes she returned with warm milk, a blanket, water and some rags. The milk was literally forced down my throat as I gagged and choked and fought back this interruption to my peaceful demise. In the meantime there was a kind of rapport established between my mother and this woman, who was earnestly trying to save my life. Eventually she brought some food for my brother and mother and kept us informed regarding the developments of our fate. Mother kept heaping praises on the woman for her kindness.

The woman's news was not exactly encouraging. It was decided that we were to be handed over to the Germans, but with an interesting twist to our fate. The Germans were to be brought here so that the community could witness our execution. Yes, we were to add excitement to their drab lives. In the meantime, the woman did her utmost to revive me so that I could face my executioners on my feet. It was sheer madness but we were grateful for every hour that passed and we all were still alive. Several days must have passed since our capture and internment in this shack. I regained my strength and my fever went down with the help of food, compresses and the blanket. The woman brought her husband, who informed us that we were 'lucky, dirty Jews', because the man whom they had sent to bring the Germans, had returned without finding any. Now they would have to decide how to dispose of us without the benefit of ingratiating themselves with the Germans over such a prize. In any case, he assured us, it would be all over by tomorrow. Thus comforting us, he took his wife by the arm and began to depart, but Mother was not ready to give up. With a show of great humility she asked the man if he would permit her the pleasure of thanking him and his wife for saving my life. Although he had nothing to do with it, she made sure that he received most of the long list of praises, concluding that he must be a very wise man to choose such an angel for a wife. My brother and I joined in the chorus, of course, and I went over, wobbly, and kissed their hands. The man was dumbstruck and obviously impressed by mother's eloquence and our display of obeisance. Something was bothering him and he asked us, finally, what kind of Jews we were. The point of that question was not clear to my mother, but she quickly replied that we were the best kind of Ukrainian Jews: that we really had nothing to do with the killing of Christ, although it was true, maybe wrongly so, that we did not believe in him. It took the man a few minutes to digest Mother's words and we thought that there might be a chance to bargain for our lives, but his reply was astonishing: 'It is fated for the Jews to suffer and die and I will not interfere with God's will.' Mother was in no position to argue with the man over that inbred anti-Semitic statement and moved to another tactic, reminding them of their kindness in saving my life and of the rewards that were awaiting them for this deed. It had worked with the old man, who did not know that we were Jewish, but in this case the man just shrugged it off by saying, 'Saving the life of a Jew boy does not count for anything.' He ended the conversation by literally dragging his wife from the shed and bolting the door.

Once again, the prospect of death was hanging over our heads and we were drained of any hope or action which would alter this course. Our eyes were dry of tears, there were no words of comfort and we were resigned to the inevitable. Evening came and we dreaded the passage of the night, knowing what the morning would bring. We heard the door open and the woman came in uttering one word: *'V'yetchera'* (supper). She left some food for us and quickly departed, anxiously avoiding becoming engaged in any conversation. In spite of everything, we managed to satisfy our hunger silently, and went to sleep. Hours later, we heard the door open and saw the outline of the man standing in the doorway. He looked around the shack and, without a word, went over to a spot and picked up what looked like a wooden club. We assumed that this was the tool with which he was going to finish us off and we set up a wail. Swearing at us, foul-mouthed, he told us to keep quiet as he went over to the door, pried open one of the boards, dropped the club, went outside and bolted the door. We went over to examine what he had done and discovered that the loose board offered us an exit. Within minutes, taking the blanket with us, we were outside, running for our lives.

'ADELE, WHERE IS YOUR HUSBAND?'

It took a long time before we could relax and savor the feeling of euphoria at having cheated death once again. In a brief space of time we had repeatedly experienced this sensation of facing death, and could have perished many times. The impact of these experiences, for me, was to realize that our lives hung precariously by a thread, in a world where few cared if we lived and most wanted us dead. It was the forest, once again, which offered us relative safety after the long hours of fear that accompanied us while traveling in the open. Every sound which could be associated with human beings – the barking of dogs, lowing of cows, bleating of sheep or the echo of a human voice – represented a danger to our existence. The forest was reassuringly silent and we entered it gratefully to catch our breath and rest our weary bones. After a while, the familiar sounds of dawn in the forest began, and since we were not asleep but had rested, Mother suggested that we should continue walking. It was wiser to do our walking during the day, under the protection of the forest. In daylight we noticed some berry bushes along the road and we picked them clean. When we could not find any more berries on the road, we moved off the path, in search of them, in the woods. Without realizing it, we strayed quite far from the road, until we were satiated with berries, but when we began to look for the path, we discovered that we were lost and were probably moving in circles. This was the second time we had found ourselves in a similar predicament. We had already learned our first important lesson: that one must take precautions to be able to get out. We began by learning how to mark our route. There was no reason to become alarmed, since we had plenty of time and were confident that eventually we would extricate ourselves. What became confusing, now that we were aware of the usefulness of leaving marks, was the fact that we came across signs that were definitely not the ones we had left behind. We discovered broken branches that were too sturdy for us to have managed, and then we discovered footprints which were certainly not ours. Under the circumstances, however, we began to follow this newfound track instead of looking for the path which we had left previously. We suddenly heard the sound of human voices and instinctively fell to the ground, our hearts beating at the impending danger. There was no lack of cover, but from the volume of the sound, we were too close for comfort.

After listening carefully, we could discern words, and the language in which they were spoken was Russian,, to our great relief. We knew that many Jews had opted to speak Russian instead of Ukrainian because they were more attached to it, but we were careful not to approach them until we heard them speaking in Yiddish as well. Our last encounter with a group like this was not exactly joyous, but our desire to meet with other Jews was overwhelming. We stood up and, careful not to startle them and thereby catch a bullet, we began to yell, '*Yidden! Yidden!*' (Jews, in Yiddish). To make doubly sure we added, '*Yivreyee*' (Jews, in Russian). Maybe our welcome would have been less favorable, if one of the men had not immediately recognized my mother. It was a heart-warming sight, finally to see someone receive us with open arms, laughter and tears of joy. The man was from Ratno and he was a friend of my parents, and he immediately asked: 'Adele, where is your husband?' He looked behind us as if expecting my father to appear. Mother, sadly and tearfully, told him that as far as she knew, Father was in the *olam habah* (the next world) with the rest of the martyrs of Ratno. The man's response to Mother's statement was a shock to us because he laughed and mercifully did not keep us in suspense, since he was delighted to be the bearer of glad tidings. He blurted out, 'Adele, you are wrong! Mordechai Leib is alive!' I will always remember that heady feeling, the thrill of excitement that raced through my being, the sensation that my heart was not big enough to retain so much joy as I ran to embrace the man. All of us embraced him and each other as we laughed and cried, shouted and danced uncontrollably, and kept repeating these actions until we were told by someone to keep the noise down. With our faces still radiating the excitement of our hearts we sat down to listen to the details of the man's story. It was very brief. He was one of the five men who were rounded up together with Father. The order was given, by one of the two Germans, for them to lie down in the street. They shot the Besht, because he pleaded to be taken to the communal grave; then Father wrenched the rifle from the soldier's hand and brought it down on the second soldier, and ran. This man took advantage of the situation and followed my father, but could not keep up with him. He wanted Father to join him in making their escape through the marshes, with which he was familiar, and yelled after him, but Father headed like a locomotive for the river. When the man saw our crestfallen faces – because we knew that Father did not know how to swim – he quickly assured us that he was certain Father had escaped. After having seen him in action, the man was sure that nothing could have thwarted Father's determination to survive

REVIVED HOPE IN OUR HEARTS AND GREATER DETERMINATION FOR SURVIVAL

These were very comforting words, and bearing in mind that there were two signs indicating that Father was alive – Mother's dream and now this man's story – we were not about to give up hope. The only question was whether our assumption that he would head for Kortiless was correct. Mother discussed this point with the man and he whole-heartedly corroborated her plan, adding that this was the only realistic option available to us. He informed Mother that in case she entertained the idea of remaining with his group, it would not be possible, because of us. We had noticed that there was not one child amongst them and the reason was obvious. Under the existing circumstances, children were a hindrance to the process of survival. It was a terrible feeling to be considered a burden, but we lived at a time of the survival of the fittest. This was a time when only the strong and able-bodied stood a chance of living for another day. This was a time when only the present was crucial. Children, who were part of the future, had to be avoided because they represented a risk which would endanger that present.

Mother brusquely told the man that unless the group was heading for Kortiless, she had no intention of remaining with it. He looked uncomfortable and tried to explain that it was the group's intention to become a fighting force which would avenge the death of Jewish children, women and men. Looking at this motley crew, it was difficult to picture them as our avengers. There was only one man with a rifle and maybe because of it he seemed to enjoy a certain amount of authority. The others held on to sticks and some sharp implements. Mother simply remarked that it would be wiser to make the effort to save the life of a child, and a good beginning would be to see if he could find us some food: as for vengeance, that could wait for God. The man managed to bring us a dish that looked like stew but turned out to be boiled mushrooms, which we ate with our hands. It lacked any describable taste except for blandness, but it filled our stomachs. While we ate, we obtained, for the first time, clear directions to Kortiless. He was certain that we could reach it in a day or two. He also told us that they intended to move out when it became dark and if we wanted to, we could join them, because for at least part of the way they would be going in the same direction. This was very acceptable to us and we decided to rest before the journey. When Mother woke us from a deep sleep, we were cranky and slow moving, while the adults were ready within minutes to march. From the beginning we fell behind and after a while Mother gave up her efforts in urging us to maintain the pace set by the adults. We were left hopelessly far behind. We continued to march, however, until we suddenly heard shots ahead of us.

There was no room for speculation as to what these shots signified and at whom they were being fired. They lasted for a number of minutes and they could not have come from the single rifle in our group's possession. We quickly moved off the path, sat down in the safety of the woods and waited. Eventually we heard the sounds of approaching footsteps and picked up some of the conversation, which was not in German but Ukrainian and Russian. These must have been the adversaries who mistakenly attacked our group and as we learned later, incidents like this happened quite frequently.

UNINVITED BEDFELLOWS

Although I was very tired, a terrible itch and stinging constantly interrupted my sleep, as if I were lying on an ant nest. Several times during the night, I awakened Mother and complained to her about it, but there was nothing she could do in the dark, and she told me that I was imagining things and that neither she nor my brother felt any ants. As soon as there was enough light, I began to look for the ants but there were none to be found. Mother helped me look for them and then she looked at my body and gasped. There were marks all over me, and then in the folds of my clothes she found lice. She became frantic and cried bitterly and quickly woke up my brother, who looked at her in confusion as she checked his body and his clothes for signs of lice. Having done that, she checked herself as well. Evidently the lice took a particular fancy to me, which was strange because lice and bed bugs are social animals, which make no distinctions and do not possess an ounce of snobbery. It puzzled Mother for a while but then she figured it out, saying, 'It's the blanket!' Upon closer inspection of the blanket, which was given to me during my illness, it became clear that this was indeed the source, and since we had not had ample opportunity to be close together for any length of time, my brother and mother were not, as yet, infected.

Lice, bed bugs and other parasites were not an unknown affliction in Kortiless, particularly amongst the Ukrainian farmers living around it. These things, however, never stood a chance in my house. 'Cleanliness is next to Godliness', Mother always said. She took this adage very seriously by subjecting us, the house and everything in it to a constant test of this *mitzvah* (good deed), and my brother and I frequently received healthy portions of it, because she continually scrubbed us with big, yellow-colored bars of awful-smelling soap. Most likely, some of those parasites received a taste of it and, concluding that they were no match for the yellow soap, decided to shun our house. Even during the most difficult times, when there was no food to put on the table, the table-cloth was clean. Now, alas, here we were without soap or water, but that did not stop Mother. She told us to get up; I carried the blanket because Mother was visibly repulsed by the idea of touching it, and we began our search through the woods for water. Finally we found a little stream, which conveniently revealed some rocks. Mother instructed me to spread out the blanket and submerge it under the water, but the thing floated. Evidently all its passengers were good rowers. I helped to sink it with the aid of some stones, and when it had absorbed sufficient water it stayed down. Next, I was told to strip, and my clothes received the same treatment as the blanket, before mother told me to come and kneel beside her. I began to protest, but one cannot protest too much when one's head is under water. She kept me under long enough to give my hair a good soaking, and with her fingers and nails massaged and scrubbed and rinsed and repeated the process, and when she was finished with my head, she did the same for the rest of my body. After I felt that I had received a new skin and nearly shriveled in the process, Mother took off her blouse and wiped me with it and told me to stay in the sun. Luckily, it was a warm summer day. She then turned her attention to my clothes and went over every inch, beating them with a rock, rinsing and squeezing them dry. It is a wonder they did not become threadbare. After spreading my clothes to dry, she began the same operation on my brother, who for some reason had ssumed he would escape this treatment. My mother believed in equality as far as this was concerned; no one escaped, including my mother herself. This was the first time we had washed since we ran away from the Sobbotniks, and we devoted almost an entire day to it. We felt clean and so did our stomachs. That was our first encounter with this aspect of suffering, but not the last, because in the terrible years that followed, it constantly plagued us. The instinct of human survival is so great that in desperation one adjusts to a disgusting coexistence with lice and other discomforts that one can hardly imagine being able to endure. We put on our clothes, even if some of the heavier garments still felt damp, and we began to search for food in the forest, with which to take the edge off our hunger.

'HE THAT PROVIDED US WITH OUR DAILY BREAD ...'

By the time we found the path, it was getting towards sunset: not because we were lost but because we had constantly stopped to feed on berries, mushrooms and anything else that looked edible. The raw mushrooms tasted even less appetizing than the stew we had the night before. It had been a long time since we had eaten any real food, and the fare that we had consumed in the meantime was playing havoc with our stomachs. That was only a minor discomfort, however, compared to the realization that we were heading in the direction where the shooting took place last night. We had no choice: this was the road that would take us to Kortiless and we had to follow it, despite the fear of what lay ahead. The obvious signs that we were on the spot where the shooting took place were some spent shells lying on the road. We looked for other signs like blood or bodies but we found nothing. We were relieved, of course, to find nothing, because after the shooting we expected that someone had been, hurt and the sight of wolves devouring the bodies was still fresh in our minds. We were anxious to get away from this place as fast as possible, but then we noticed a parcel lying at the side of the road. It turned out to be a bag and inside it, like a gift from God, were the remains of about half a loaf of bread. There was no doubt in my mother's mind that it was the hand of God that was involved in this miracle of supplying us with food.

Mother's concern was for us to keep moving, in the hope that by sunset we would be near some farm, so the treasure which we had just found had to wait to be devoured. The forest, which offered us a sense of security during the day, became a source of danger at night. In spite of our efforts to keep moving as fast as possible, the forest remained never-ending and as night fell, we became resigned to the inevitability of having to spend the night in its midst. We continued to march, however, but slackened our pace considerably as we neared the point of exhaustion (I in particular) and Mother decided that it would be best to stop. She noticed a big tree, a few paces from the road, and brought us over to it. I think I must have fallen asleep before I managed to consume the piece of bread which mother handed out.

'AND A PILLAR OF LIGHT SHALL LEAD YOU ...'

Mother had trouble falling asleep and maintained a vigilant eye over us. At one point she noticed that the sky was particularly bright on the horizon. It was as if the sun refused to set. With great effort she managed to wake us up in order to point out this phenomenon. It was sufficiently fascinating to jar us awake, and we quickly got up and began to walk towards the light in the sky. We soon discovered the mystery of the lights. At least two or three dwellings were on fire, and by their light we could see that it was a sizable community. Finally, here was the farm or 'civilization' which earlier we had hoped to reach. The strange thing was that nobody was trying to put out the fires and the people running around were engaged in a battle between themselves. We were now close enough to hear the cries of pain, insults and threats, and understood that we were witnessing a community conflict in the process of being resolved. We were sufficiently familiar with the behavior of Ukrainian farmers and their squabbles (which occasionally led to belligerent confrontations) to be not overly frightened by what we saw. In most cases these hostilities ended with some burned-down houses and some serious cuts and bruises. Although lethal weapons like axs and pitchforks were used, they rarely resulted in fatalities.

It was clear that we could not approach this community under the circumstances and it was doubtful whether we would have revealed ourselves in any case, bearing in mind our reception at the last village. We had no trouble circumventing this village and leaving the bloodletting behind. The road we were following was in the open and occasionally we spotted farms. When Mother felt that we had walked far enough and deserved a rest, we took refuge in some haystacks that were located not far from the road

GRANDMOTHER FREIDA IS ALIVE AND DOING WELL

The clatter of a wagon and the stomping of horses awoke us. The sounds were too close and the wagon's occupants must have seen us, so it was useless for us to run because there was no place to hide. We remained where we were, our hearts beating with fear, as the wagon approached and stopped near us. Our surprise was overwhelming when we were greeted with a polite 'Good morning'. Mother quickly told the couple driving the wagon that we were on the way to Kortiless. They were not inquisitive and they had a look of anxiety about them, but they told us that we were welcome to get on board because they were going in that direction. When we boarded the wagon, we understood the reason for the distress on the couple's faces. Two young men, badly hurt and softly groaning, were lying on the floor of the wagon. One of them was lying face down, with a deep gash on the fleshy part of his exposed behind, evidently caused by a sharp pointed stick, some of which was still imbedded in the wound. The second man was curled up, holding his limp arm: judging from its unusual position and his bloodstained shirt, a hatchet blow must have broken it. These were the couple's sons and they were the more severe casualties of last night's grievance. It seemed that the fighting was over the ownership of a parcel of land that a recently-departed patriarch had left, and the siblings had problems dividing it amongst themselves. Now the parents were taking their sons to be treated, but they seemed to be even more shaken up by the injustice. Mother's curiosity was aroused by the fact that there was someone in this area who was capable of dealing, medically, with such severe wounds, and she began to question the couple.

The answer we received was staggering and we could not believe our ears. The woman told us that there was a Jewish woman who had been administering medical treatment, and she added that everyone had heard that she managed to save many lives. This woman was confident that her boys would be patched up as good as new. From the description that the woman gave of the medical person, it sounded as if she was talking about my Grandmother. But we knew that grandmother was in Ratno during the massacre, and there seemed no way that she could have survived. Mother continued to question the woman, and when she asked her how long this 'doctor' had been in the area, the woman could not tell us: she had only recently found out about her.

Mother informed us that the terrain looked familiar to her and that we were not too far from Kortiless. Soon we stopped near a farmhouse where the doctor was supposed to be staying. We got off and waited with baited breath as the couple, pointing to the victims, explained the purpose of their visit to the man who came out to greet us. The man disappeared into the house and within a few minutes came out with my grandmother. As I consider some of the events in my life, and whether they were the result of sheer coincidence or divine intervention, I view this incident as one of those miraculous occasions where life is much stranger than fiction. When we are presented in fictional literature with a similar situation, we give it the name of *deus ex machina*. Sure enough, here was my beautiful, short, gray-haired grandmother standing before us with her familiar satchel in her hand.

Our Ukrainian disguise did not prevent her from recognizing us, the instant she saw us. She stared at us in disbelief and the shock caused her to sway unsteadily as my brother and I ran towards her yelling: '*Babbe!*' (Grandmother). After everyone understood the meaning of this strange encounter, the couple's impatient urging, for Grandmother to attend to their sons, interrupted the joy of our reunion. To illustrate the blind bigotry which infested the Ukrainians: the man who so generously had given us a lift now expressed his surprise at our being Jewish and frankly admitted that he thought he was doing it for *lyudi* (people) and not *Szydi*. This exchange took place with complete nonchalance, between the father of the two injured sons and my grandmother's host, in the presence of my brother and me. As if he had committed some transgression, the man tried to defend himself by adding that he would not have bothered to stop had he known this fact before. At the same time, my kindly Jewish grandmother, with the help of my mother, tried to patch up his mutilated sons. It took a long time and occasional screaming emanating from the house, indicating that the task was a difficult one. At one point the two men were called in to help physically restrain the man with the splinters in his behind. I must admit that the screaming did not bother me and I felt no sympathy for their predicament. The only thing which interested me was that my grandmother and my mother should soon reappear.

The women came out first, followed by the man with the broken arm. His arm was braced and tied with rags, in a manner that held it rigidly in front of him. The second man appeared, wearing a diaper instead of his pants, supported by his father as he limped painfully to the wagon. It seemed that the patients were in much better condition when they came out and aside from being uncomfortable and in pain for a while, they would survive. Their mother was very grateful and thanked my grandmother most profusely. The father expressed his gratitude to the host, as if it was he who had performed the medical treatment, and promised that within a few days he would deliver payment for the service.

Finally we could be with our Grandmother and resume the joy of the reunion. Mother had already managed to tell grandmother the wonderful news of the witness who claimed that Father had escaped the massacre. Grandmother concurred with Mother's assumption that Father would be heading in the direction of Kortiless. I changed the subject by bringing up an immediate problem: I was very hungry. For the first time since we escaped from the Sobbotniks, we enjoyed the pleasure of a warm meal and the delight of a full stomach, without having the worry of leaving something for later. As we ate, Grandmother revealed to us the circumstances that had saved her from the massacre, and her ordeal of the past few weeks. I was surprised to hear that so much time had already passed since the massacre. This was possibly because at my age, the concept of time was not a definite entity, or more likely because under the circumstances, our primary concern was the present, and the moments which lay ahead, not time which had elapsed. At the time the massacre in Ratno took place, my grandmother was away at a farm helping to deliver a baby and to save the life of its mother. The grateful farmer kept her hidden, but word of her miraculous deed spread quickly and other farmers called upon her services. Protected by them, she was transferred from one farmer to the other, as she slowly made her way in the direction of Kortiless. She had been with this present farmer for the past week and a half, not because of his generosity, but because he had realized the potential of Grandmother's talent. While she attended to the patients, he decided upon the terms of remuneration, which he kept in return for her food and shelter. It was an interesting phenomenon: a farmer who ran a medical care centre.

We stayed until the farmer began fidgeting about our presence, despite the fact that we helped around the house and worked long hours in the fields, which earned us more than our keep. But the farmer had his reputation to uphold, and harboring Jews could not only tarnish it but also land him in deep trouble. He was willing to make an exception in Grandmother's case because, after all, she was serving the public. Several times during our stay, Grandmother was taken to do house calls and she tried to find out if anyone had seen a man who answered my father's description, but she had no luck. This was not an encouraging sign: nevertheless, we reluctantly took our leave of Grandmother and told her that that she should remain where she was, and that when we found Father we would return for her. This time we knew the exact direction of Kortiless, and that it would be only a few hours of walking before we reached it. Kortiless was not going to be a haven for us, but a starting place which would lead us to Father. Towards nightfall we set out once more on the road, not without the nagging fear of having to face new dangers. We were braced by our hope and belief that the Almighty would guide our path safely.

3 A Friendly Embrace

We did not reach the village of Kortiless this time. Mother reasoned that it was unlikely that Father would seek safety there, as the reason we had abandoned Kortiless in the first place was still valid. Instead, she decided that we should begin our search with the farmers in the vicinity of Kortiless, with whom Father had business dealings prior to the arrival of the Nazis. Even in the dark she recognized a farm which looked familiar to her, and she knew its owners. She decided that we should spend what little was left of the night in a nearby haystack. In the morning, when Mother noticed activity on the farm, she awakened us and we hopefully and yet apprehensively approached the farm.

There was a woman doing some chores in the yard. Mother recognized her and called her by her name. The woman was so surprised to see Mother that the bucket she was holding fell from her hand, as she gaped at us open-mouthed. They embraced and afterwards Mother introduced us. It was comforting to feel that not everybody hated us, and nothing was more reassuring to see than a warm embrace. The woman then called for her husband to behold the surprise that awaited him. He too was delighted to see Mother and stood there scratching his head and repeating Mother's name in disbelief. I recognized the couple from the many times they had visited us in Kortiless after their Sunday church service. They and my parents were friends, and that friendship had lasted even during difficult times. They quickly invited us into the house and treated us to a greatly-appreciated breakfast, although during our stay with Grandmother, we had forgotten the terrible sensation of hunger pain.

The subject of Father came up and the woman gasped and began fidgeting. It became apparent that it was uncomfortable for both of them to talk about him. Realizing that they must have seen him, Mother began to prod them, even if she assumed that their reluctance to speak meant that they knew he was dead. The man began by saying, 'Leiba is crazy.' This declaration came as a complete surprise to us, but we listened patiently as the couple related the events of their encounter with Father, his difficulty in recognizing them, his sickness and finally his departure. They were certain that he did not fully know who they were even on the day he left for Kortiless, despite their warning that he should not go there. It took them a long time to tell the story and when they had finished, they sadly told Mother that in the condition Father was in, it was doubtful that he had a chance of surviving. When Mother inquired if Father was physically ill, the woman explained that at first he had fainted several times and slept for a long while but after about two days he got up and worked in the fields, not showing any sign of weakness. The man pointed his finger to his head and shrugged his shoulders to indicate his earlier diagnosis of Father's condition. They explained that they had tried to keep him with them, but he had insisted on going to Kortiless. If it was any comfort to us, the man added, he was certain that nothing had happened to Father in Kortiless, because he would have heard about it.

Mother could not explain or respond to their questions regarding Father's strange behavior. She told the couple that it was her intention to look for him, and if he was still alive she was certain that she would find him. Mother was determined, and they realized that there was no sense in trying to dissuade her from her purpose. They warned her to avoid Kortiless because recently the Germans had carried out a reprisal raid against the village and of course, the Jews were blamed for that too, even if by that time there was not one Jew in the area. A number of farmers in the vicinity were also named as people to be avoided.

THE SEARCH GOES ON

Towards evening, with a supply of as much non-perishable food as the couple could spare, we set out. Our immediate destination was the home of a close relative of the couple, who lived several hours of walking-time away. We reached the place about midnight and once again we waited until morning to approach the people. Although the welcome was at first restrained and on the verge of being short-lived, when Mother conveyed regards from the couple who had helped us, their attitude changed. Mother explained the purpose of our journey and asked if they had heard anything about Father's whereabouts. The answer was positive, but before we could become excited about the news, the man followed up with details that marred our excitement. He had not met up with Father personally, but he had heard about him, three or four weeks ago, and the news was that he was crazy. His advice was that it was too dangerous for us to wander around looking for Father because that increased the chances of running into someone who would kill us or hand us over to the Germans. The best thing for us to do was to stay in one place – he was even willing to put us up for a while – and if Father was still alive and sane, he would find us. Mother thanked the people for their generosity and concern for our safety, but explained that the only choice left for us was to continue looking for Father. She reasoned that if, God forbid, it was true that Father was crazy then he would not be looking for us: consequently his safety depended on her finding him as quickly as possible. If the stories of his state of mind were exaggerated, however, as she believed they were, then the safety of the four of us depended on finding each other. The urgency of finding Father made Mother even bolder and we did not wait for the cover of darkness to continue our search. After receiving some suggestions as to the probable places that Father might be hiding, if he were still alive, we left.

We were welcomed with varying degrees of civility by some of the farmers we approached. There were those who greeted us with outright hostility, ordering us to leave and adding that they had assumed they were finally rid of all Jews and that we should be grateful they did not put an end to our miserable existence. Possibly the only reason they did not do so was because they knew Mother from a time when human beings behaved with compassion towards the unfortunate. Fortunately, there were also those who received us gladly, expressing sympathy for our plight and offering advice and even shelter for a night. With the talent of a great detective, Mother gathered every bit of information about father, considered the various possibilities and chose a path of action. It became quite clear that we must avoid going to Kortiless because of the recent German reprisal raid there, about which we had already been told.

OUR PERSEVERANCE IS REWARDED

After a number of days of wandering, we found ourselves in the vicinity of where we once had our farm. 'God smiled upon us and rewarded our perseverance and trust in Him.' These were the words uttered by my mother as she surveyed the surroundings. We noticed that some farmhouses had been burned to the ground. Mother knew the people who used to live there and told us that this must be the outcome of a 'neighborly misunderstanding'. She decided to move on, but when she noticed that the destruction was too great to be the result of a feud, she abandoned that theory. At one point we saw some people in the process of rebuilding their house and we decided to approach them. The people recognized Mother and the reception was overwhelming. When she asked what had happened, the answer was one word which explained everything: *'Nyemtsee'* (Germans). As she began to pursue the question of Father's whereabouts, they smiled and eagerly, almost as a chorus, answered that he was here. He had been helping them build the house but since today was *Sobbota* (Saturday), he had refused to join them. They pointed in the direction of where he was staying, saying: *'On tam'* (He's there).

My brother and I took off with the speed of jackrabbits in the direction of the barn that was pointed out to us. Mother yelled after us and told us to wait. She feared that it would not be exactly beneficial to Father if we were to barge in on him in our state of excitement. This request for restraint was strange, after all the time of hoping and anticipation of this moment, but we did as we were told. Our hearts beating and filled with joy to the point of eruption, we allowed Mother to precede us as we carefully approached the barn. Even from the outside we heard Father's sweet voice engaged in reciting prayers.

When we entered the barn, it was a shock to us to discover Father fast asleep while clearly chanting, with intermittent stops, some liturgical melody. It had become a source of amusement in my family, that for poor Father, the day was not long enough to pray three times, recite psalms and study daily portions of the Torah, so he had to make up for it at night. He denied doing it, of course, but in case it was true, he would make sure to fasten his yarmulke before he went to sleep. Mother would awaken him from these impromptu concerts by reminding him that this was a time for sleeping and not praying.

The three of us stood there observing him, as tears of joy streamed down our faces and our throats were choked with emotion. He sensed our presence, opened his eyes and immediately shut them again and covered his face with his hands. Mother gently called out his name, 'Mordechai Leib', but my brother and I could not contain ourselves any longer and we pounced on him yelling: *'Tatte! Tatte!'* (Father). He was certain that this was no dream as he stood up, holding each one of us under an arm, and went over to embrace Mother.

There are no words that can describe accurately an event like the 'revival of the dead' or the 'arrival of the Messiah'. Rather, there is no lack of words, but it is those particular words that can convey the entire message that become hard to find. In our case it was a situation where actions speak louder than words. During our quest for Father, I had imagined various circumstances under which our reunion might take place and the stories we would have to tell each other. The stories and words would have to wait. No one spoke. We sat for a long time on the floor, huddled together, holding on to each other, allowing the reality of the situation to penetrate. From time to time a new flood of tears of joy came pouring out, as one of us would make the effort to begin to speak. It took a long time for that to happen, and when finally Mother began to talk, she first told Father that his mother was alive. Father was silent as he listened to a few of the barest details of our encounter with Grandmother and where she was. He lifted his head, closed his eyes and said, 'Thank you, Creator of the universe', and went outside, with us at his heels. He washed himself and made us do the same and then began the morning prayer, while we stood beside him, occasionally mouthing passages that we already knew by heart. When he finished, we ate some of the meager provisions we had with us, and then we began relating the events of the past six weeks, since we had last seen each other in Ratno. There were two interruptions, both for the purpose of reciting prayers. Prayers were always for him the first priority and obligation. Nothing could ever take precedence over that. When he had recited the last prayer, Maariv, it is actually the first prayer ushering in the following day, and Shabbes was over, Father took command of the situation. He announced that the first thing we would do would be to find Grandmother.

HAIL TO THE NEW COMMANDER

It was an amazing thing for me to observe the transformation that took place in my mother. For six weeks she had had to make every decision and calculate every step in order for us to stay alive, a responsibility which she had carried out with determination and wisdom and which had left me in awe of her ability. Her lack of enthusiasm for Father's plan soon became apparent, as she raised the question of what we would do once we joined Grandmother. He had no answer, except for a Yiddish expression that says, 'God will worry about tomorrow.' This was a common reply amongst Jews but it did not satisfy Mother, and she insisted that unless a more practical solution was worked out, she would not budge from this place. We stayed exactly a week, during which the farmer's house, that father was helping to build, was completed, and the farmer began dropping hints about the fact that our staying with him was not too healthy for him and his family. Word was bound to get around and the Bulbovtsi or the Germans would not take too kindly to his harboring Jews. He was sorry, of course, and made some suggestions about other farmers who might help us, but he had his own family to think of. During this week, my parents had tried to work out a plan of how we were going to survive with winter quickly approaching, and their conclusion was a shattering one. There was no possible plan that we could make to ensure our future, because for us there was only a present and an annihilated past. The only way we could survive was to deal with situations in the best possible manner as they arose. Armed with this bitter lesson and with the food that the farmer could spare, we set out to retrieve Grandmother.

It was an entirely different situation now that Father was in the lead: not that I did not have complete confidence in mother, but with me on my Mother's back and my brother on my father's, walking distances became a different experience. Within a number of hours we were at the house where grandmother was staying. The world had become smaller. Once again we waited until morning to see Grandmother, and we slept soundly knowing that Father was there to watch over us.

I had already experienced the emotional upheaval that a reunion with a loved one could create. Yet I could not stand by stoically and observe the meeting of my father and my grandmother and not be drawn into shedding tears of joy at the sight. After the excitement of the reunion subsided, and we were enjoying the breakfast which the farmer offered us, he made sure to clarify the point that there was no room for another four Jews on his farm. Father thanked the man for his hospitality and added that that he would be glad to relieve him of the burden of caring for Grandmother. Realizing that this meant an end to his medical service and the income which it brought, the man tried to suggest some compromise whereby Grandmother would continue her service and we would be hidden somewhere. Father did not trust the greedy man and was certain that at the first opportunity he would dispose of us, either by leaking our whereabouts to the Germans, or even more easily, by getting some Ukrainian thugs to do the dirty work. When Father once again thanked him for his kind offer, but said that it was his intention to head towards Kortiless, the man showed his true colors and belligerently told us to clear out of his house immediately. Grandmother quickly grabbed her bag and whatever apparel she had accumulated, and we were once again on the road, exposed to new dangers that awaited us.

WHERE DO WE RUN TO NOW?

The first objective was to get as far away as possible from the farmer who had just lost his 'medical services' and might get it into his head to organize a hunting party for us. We were now a conspicuous party of five, and even if our parents could carry the two of us boys, there was also Grandmother, who impeded our progress. Father began scanning the area for a place to hide out until nightfall, because to walk in broad daylight on the road was to invite additional trouble, aside from our possible pursuer. Suddenly father noticed a potato field which was in the process of being picked, but since it was Sunday there was no one there, so he motioned us to follow him. After a few minutes he found what he was looking for: a big hole in the ground almost filled with potatoes and covered with straw to prevent them from turning green in the sun. Quickly we lowered ourselves into the hole and disappeared from view.

We had plenty of time to wait and to contemplate our situation. The immediate question was where we would go when nightfall came. A complete and thorough analysis of the situation took place, with the three adults piecing together bits of information to obtain the full picture. To begin with, Father explained that Kortiless, including the church, was almost completely razed to the ground as part of the German reprisal for Partisan and Bulbovtsi activity in the area. Our joining the Partisans, who were on the Russian side of the war effort, was out of the question. To begin with, they accepted only able-bodied men. My brother and I did not exactly fit into that category, even if Grandmother's medical knowledge could be of great assistance to them. Secondly, at this point the Partisans were not a well-organized force but one which consisted primarily of small, disgruntled and ill-led Ukrainian groups. They were not willing to accept Jews into their ranks and in fact were not averse to killing Jews, to mollify their own frustrations or just for the fun of it. To further complicate the situation there were the Bulbovtsi, who posed a greater danger to the remaining Jews in rural areas than the Germans. They derived their name from Tarass Bulba, a one-time Ukrainian nationalist. This group consisted primarily of collaborators with the Germans, on the latter's promise that they would set up an autonomous Ukrainian state. The Germans had no intention of satisfying these Ukrainian aspirations. In fact, as their success on the Russian front grew, they made it clear that a free Ukrainian state was not part of their plan of world domination.

When the German advance was finally halted – and in fact

they began to retreat – they took precautions to disarm the ethnic militias and to kill the more prominent leaders. To sum up the situation: the Germans were fighting the Partisans and the Bulbovtsi, the Partisans were fighting Bulbovtsi; and the Germans; the Bulbovtsi were fighting the Germans and the Partisans; and they were all killing Jews.

Our options were obviously very limited. We could remain where we were, be killed by the Ukrainians or handed over to the Germans. We could return to the vicinity of Kortiless and try our luck with the hospitality of our 'friends' or move into the forest (there were large forests near Kortiless). Father's knowledge of survival in the forest, however, was practically non-existent. With winter approaching, without food and shelter, we were certain to perish there. It was decided that we should try and reach another village, larger than Kortiless, by the name of Mokran.

ON THE ROAD TO MOKRAN

There was a Jewish community there, and to the best of our knowledge, there had been as yet no massacre. My parents had relatives in the village and we hoped that they would help us. After all, Jews stick together in good and bad times. As for bad times, they could not possibly be worse. We accepted the fact that we would not exactly be welcomed with open arms to share in what little they possessed, but we had no other choice. The misery to which Jews were subjected caused the struggle for survival to have a dehumanizing effect. Father was familiar with the territory because he used to trade in the area and knew perfectly the way to Mokran. Now all we had to do was wait for darkness to begin our journey.

Sometimes events occur in one's life that are so strange that divine intervention or providence remain the only possible explanations. I was so frequently exposed to these manifestations that they became part of my belief. It is true that today there are many times when I wonder: if there are such things,

113

why do they not still occur? Maybe it is because I am no longer a religious man – that is, in the sense of observance. I do believe in the existence of God.

Father recited Maariv and then T'filat Haderech (a prayer for the traveler) and we climbed out of the hole. There was a full moon and, comforted by the fact that we had reached a clear decision, we hoped that, with God's help, we would safely reach our destination. According to Father, we would reach Mokran well before dawn, so we could unobtrusively sneak into the village and hide with one of our relatives. We had been marching for many hours. At times we were forced to make detours because of farmhouses that were too close to the road, where dogs, who sensed our presence, began to bark. It would not be exactly advantageous to our safety to meet up with an angry Ukrainian, roused from a deep sleep by the barking of his dogs. Finally the road reached a section in which it penetrated a large forest. Father was ecstatic, as he explained that now we were safe, because this forest would continue for about ten kilometers and after that was the village. To ease our burden, he told us stories of how he had traveled this road before, and of the time when he managed to escape, on horseback, from highwaymen who tried to rob him and his companions.

A large forest at night is a scary place to be, for a 6-year-old child. We had managed to survive the experience with Mother, however, and now that Father was with us, I certainly breathed with relief. Compared with the open countryside, with real and imaginary danger suggested by every sound, we finally felt safe. The trees cut off the light of the moon, by this time lower on the horizon, and it was becoming dark. Sound in the forest travels great distances, especially on a cold night such as this. Suddenly we heard the sound of voices and marching approaching us. We immediately took off into the forest, as far away from the road as possible, grateful that we did not meet up with these people in the open countryside. Whoever they were, one thing was certain: they were not our friends.

Finally the intruding noise of their footsteps and voices

subsided, and the forest returned to the stillness of the night. We began to move back in the direction of the road that we had abandoned before, but it was as if the road had disappeared from the face of the earth. It seemed so obvious that all we had to do to find the road was to move in the direction from which the noise of the footsteps had come, but we seemed to be moving in circles. Every time we reached a clearing which looked like a road, it eventually brought us to a dead end. Mother became upset and argumentative and even taunted Father with the fact that for six weeks she had wandered with us, even part of the time in strange territory, and never got lost. This was not exactly true; we had had our share of walking around in circles in broad daylight, but we kept silent and did not take sides. To ease the tension, it was decided that the best thing to do was to sit down to relax and get some food into our systems. Only when daylight came did we finally stumble upon the road, which was not more than about a hundred meters from where we sat down to rest.

FATHER FINDS A SAVIOR

Father could not explain why he had not managed to find the road last night, so he shrugged his shoulders and added, 'It's God's will … Besides, there is no sense in becoming upset and Mokran will not run away, and we will reach it tonight.' This was for Mother's benefit. In the meantime we were safe and walking on the road which was to lead us to Mokran. We came to the end of the forest by about the middle of the day and we settled down for a rest. Father informed us that he intended to go alone to ask at the nearby farms for some news about Mokran and also to see if he could obtain some more food. We still had some, but this was a commodity of which we could never claim to have enough. We were opposed to his scouting mission, but Father decided it was necessary and we certainly could not do it together.

Hours later Father returned with food, accompanied by a

Ukrainian man named Adam, and his wife. My parents knew the couple well. They were from our area of Kortiless and in fact it was from Adam's brother, or some other relative, that my parents rented the farm. While Mother and Grandmother were conversing with the couple, we were demolishing some of the food which Father had brought. He immediately became busy reciting the prayers of Mincha (afternoon prayer) and Birkat Hagomel (prayer for being saved from a calamity). It was true that we faced danger every day and it was a miracle that we had managed to survive this far, but before this incident Father had never added the prayer of Birkat Hagomel. When we stopped eating and paid attention to the conversation of the adults, conducted in Ukrainian, we discovered the reason. Adam told us that the Jews of Mokran were massacred that morning. Had we not lost our way, and reached Mokran this morning as planned, we would have been amongst the victims. Without gloating, Father pointed out that it was divine intervention and not his lack of sense of direction which made us wander aimlessly last night for hours, about a hundred meters from the road.

INTO THE WOODS OR DIE

Our joy at surviving another calamity was short-lived, because once again we were faced with the problem of what to do next. It was clear that the Germans were now eliminating, systematically and totally, all Jewish communities, and what they missed, the Ukrainian bandits were finishing. It was obvious that there was no shelter for us in the arms of 'civilization' and that the forest was our only possible sanctuary. That brought us back to our earlier conclusion that, essentially, there was no chance of our survival for any length of time. Mother was devastated and began to cry bitterly, as she wondered out loud if it would not have been better if we had reached Mokran, so that by now all the worries and suffering which lay ahead of us would have been over and done with.

It was Adam who came to the rescue, in more ways than one. To begin with, he was quite gruff with Mother and silenced her wailing. The man was fond of us and full of admiration of the fact that we had managed to survive thus far. It took courage and strength to continue with the struggle, and from what he had heard from Father about our experiences, he was certain that we possessed these qualities. We were his favorite *Szydi* and he was not about to let us perish at the hands of Germans or his countrymen. We were to join him and his wife and head in the direction of the forest near Kortiless, and set ourselves up for the winter. His speech left us in awe but his last declaration was like the coming of the Messiah. We were eager to hear what reason a Ukrainian farmer would have to be hiding out with us in the forest.

Adam was at least ten years older than my father and one of his two sons served in the Russian army. Unlike most Ukrainians who deserted when the Russians retreated, he had stayed on. This automatically labeled Adam and his family as Russian sympathizers and he became a target of Kolya's abuse, which he courageously managed to ward off. When Kolya tried to conscript Adam's young son into becoming one of his henchmen and the lad refused, Kolya threatened to send him off to a forced labor detail for being a communist. The 17-year-old boy joined the Partisans and was killed in an encounter with Germans in the vicinity of Kortiless. Adam was a marked man and so were the families of the other casualties, who were identified by collaborators. Adam anticipated German reprisal and so he and his wife decided to seek refuge in the area of Mokran. When the Germans came with a prepared list of people for execution, they discovered that most of the people on the list had taken precautions not to be around. Not to feel thwarted and outwitted, however, and to provide the mission with a sense of accomplishment, they simply increased their quota of carnage by eliminating most of the village, including the church, from the face of the earth. Adam was now a man hunted by the Germans as well as the Ukrainians of Kortiless. The latter blamed him, and of course the Jews, for offering the Germans a reason for their blood-thirsty deed. The world knows, of course, that the Nazis never needed an excuse for their mindless killings.

Adam finished his long and detailed account of the hectic events in his life since we had last seen him. Then he added with a smile, 'As Leiba would say, it is the will of *Boshze* [God] that we should meet again, under these terrible circumstances.' He was not a devout Christian and the statement was made to poke fun, good-naturedly, at my father, who at that moment was busy reciting Maariv. Then Adam mentioned the essential articles we would need in order to set ourselves up in the forest. It was not a long list, but he may as well have mentioned the moon, because it included: an ax, pots for cooking, eating utensils, blankets and above all tobacco. The last item was odd for us, but Adam was a heavily-addicted smoker and the lack of tobacco became a source of tension and despair later on. When Father offered the opinion that no one would willingly part with these articles, Adam agreed, but laughingly added: 'We won't ask them.' Adam's presence and confidence introduced new hope into our lives. At a time when the situation looked so bleak that the gaping jaws of death were beginning to close upon us, hope was a 'gift from God' and Adam was His messenger who delivered it to us.

FOREST ARCHITECTURE AND LORE

There were seven of us now as we started for our destination – although not before Father recited T'filat Haderech, for which Adam had no patience, so he began to walk ahead with his wife. He maintained the lead and set a pace which left us way behind. From the outset, he made it abundantly clear that he was not our guardian, and that if we were going to stay together, everyone had to pull their own weight. This was a time for discipline and not for weaklings or crybabies: as he finished his statement, he looked pointedly at me, saying *'panyemayesh!'* (understand), instead of the plural form, *'panyemayetyee'*. For good reasons, he probably assumed me to be the weak link in his plans. Only when we approached a farm would Adam wait until we caught up with him. Then, while we rested in safety, he and Father would stealthily search for articles that would be beneficial to us. Father had much to learn about stealth and stealing. Even if our lives depended on the success of these qualities, he found it abhorrent and demeaning. Nevertheless, he adjusted to the reality of our existence, and Adam was a good teacher, if at times ruthless.

The farmers, conscious of the fact that theft was part of life, left very little in the yards to be stolen. If anything was left, there were also a number of dogs to prevent thieves. By the time we reached our destination – the forest in the vicinity of Kortiless – we were still short of many of the things on the original list of items, but we did have a hatchet, a small cooking pot that Adam took from a pigsty, some wearing apparel and rags. After choosing a spot in the forest and telling us that this was his, Adam told us to pick our own place. If this was all there was to it, it was very disappointing, but we chose a spot about twenty meters away and dejectedly sat down. Then I noticed Adam take off with the hatchet into the forest, and I followed him to learn more about the lessons of survival. He looked around and saw some tall, young birch saplings, and with hefty blows began to cut them down. Never more than two or three in the same spot, so as not to leave telltale spaces. My brother and Father joined us and after Adam had about twenty saplings we helped to drag them back to our site. He stripped the branches from about eight saplings of equal size, sharpened the points on both ends, stuck them into the ground and created eight arches in a row. Then he wove the remaining smaller saplings through the arches, pushing them into the ground at one of the openings. Within a short time there was a sturdy U frame. The branches from the saplings were carefully interwoven into the frame and on top of that Adam placed many large ferns that

119

we helped him gather. All this was done with a minimal amount of words. 'Look and learn', he said, and that is exactly what we did. We were amazed to see that within a matter of several hours he had set up a shelter, and then he handed Father the ax. He did not help us, except for giving occasional criticism, as we tried in vain to emulate his accomplishment. Our shelter had to be at least twice the size of his, and even after working until dark, we had a poor imitation of his masterpiece. The knowledge that a shelter of this kind could be set up, however, was of great comfort. Perfection would come later.

The things that we had to learn about living in the forest were endless. Almost every action needed forethought and consideration of what effect it would have. Some of the rules we learned by applying common sense, others the hard way, through experience, and the rest by stern admonitions from Adam. To begin with, since it concerned the safety of us all, we were warned by Adam not to disturb the foliage around the campsite and to avoid creating paths by treading the same course frequently. Going to the bathroom meant going far from the site and always to the same designated place. This habit was not only for sanitation purposes, such as reducing flies and mosquitoes, but also to prevent wild boar – which could at times be dangerous – from developing the habit of attaching themselves to our site when they came to demolish our excretions. My brother and I were frequently and sternly warned not to wander from the campsite – not that we had any intention of doing it. At first the idea itself that home was this campsite in the forest was difficult for me to accept. As time passed, however, and our knowledge of the forest increased, I grew to realize that it was not our enemy but in fact our shield.

We spent the next two days fixing up our shelter and becoming acquainted with the immediate area around the site. There was water near by and Mother, Grandmother and Adam's wife got busy washing themselves, our clothes and us. Then the men took their turn. On the first day, Adam showed us how to make a fire. We had no matches, but he had an apparatus, which he carried in a little pouch tied to his waist, called a *smekalka*. First he gathered some dried grass and then, took out from his pouch a small flintstone, dried fungus and a piece of metal. He placed a piece of the fungus on the edge of the stone and held them between his thumb and forefinger, and struck the stone with the piece of metal. There were many sparks and soon the piece of fungus began to smolder, and he placed it in the dried grass. Then, as he swung it in a large circle, the grass caught fire. In his stern manner, Adam warned us that during the day we must never use freshly-cut wood, because it creates smoke, and that is detectable for great distances, whereas at night it is preferable to use green wood because the smoke keeps away mosquitoes. The first part certainly sounded logical but as for the mosquitoes, evidently not all of them agreed with him, because they plagued us without mercy – but away from the bonfire it was even worse.

The food supply that we had brought with us began to dwindle. Father and Adam decided to go foraging for food, at the farms within closest proximity. As was his usual custom, Father recited 'T'filat Haderech' and Adam armed himself with the ax. They set out towards the evening. The feeling of comparative safety, which I previously attributed to the forest, seemed to disappear with the departure of the two men. To be left alone with three women and a not-much-older brother for protection in this gigantic forest was not exactly my idea of safety. I could not confess my fear to anyone. My brother would laugh at me and Mother would assure me that everything would be fine and there was nothing to fear. To go to sleep in the shelter was out of the question, so I joined my brother near the bonfire: it was his job to maintain it the whole night. The dancing flames of the fire cast frightening, moving shadows around us and my heart would jump at these apparitions and at occasional sounds emanating from the depth of the forest. Yet I held on and not once did I cry out. When Mother insisted that we should go to bed, my brother replied that he wanted to wait for Father and I eagerly seconded that idea. My brother started a custom that night, which we maintained throughout our many vigils for Father's return from his forays in the quest for food. There were four potatoes left. My brother took a stick, spitted one of the potatoes on it and rotated it near the hot coals, avoiding the flame to prevent the formation of soot. Then he carefully peeled and ate a thin layer and repeated the process. I joined him in this activity and the two potatoes each kept us busy for many hours, at the same time mollifying our hunger. With the birth of dawn, the birds, chirped happily to greet its arrival and my heart could join them, with joy at the sight of my father and Adam returning – the same heart which had experienced a very bad night, learning the terrible lesson of dealing with the sensation of fear. There was only one way of overcoming fear: by accepting the fact that it was there and learning to contend with it. There is no shame in being afraid, just as there is no glory in being proud.

The food Father brought consisted primarily of potatoes, stolen from the fields, and a small bag of assorted pieces of bread. But the real treasure was a pot in which to cook those potatoes. He also managed to bring two whole spoons and one 'half' spoon, which was broken in half at the scoop part. We used to take turns at using it, to eat the potato soup, which was tasteless because there was nothing to add to it. Salt was an unobtainable commodity. The potatoes were boiled in their skins and everything was consumed. As long as there were potatoes and other vegetables in the fields, Father avoided asking for handouts and used his calls on various farmers as 'social visits' to establish relations for future needs. It was not a question of pride but of good politics. Father knew most of the farmers he and Adam visited, but in some cases Adam waited, hidden, outside. The farmers could understand why Leiba, a Jew, was reduced to this kind of existence,but Adam, a Ukrainian, carried on his shoulders the guilt of being responsible for the massacre of the 'God-fearing Christians' of Kortiless and the adjoining area. Even though Father was younger and stronger than Adam, he had to carry food for five people, whereas Adam had to carry food for only two. The only way Adam would help him carry the food was if Father was lucky enough to obtain some tobacco with which to bribe him.

Despite the fact that the food was doled out carefully, to make it last as long as possible, and was supplemented with any available berries and mushrooms, our supply ran out before Adam's. The first couple of times, Adam was cajoled and entreated to join Father, with the promise that Father would try to get him tobacco, but when he did not succeed, Adam became belligerent, owing to withdrawal symptoms, and Father had to make the journey alone. Adam's raving and hostile moods were a matter of grave concern and we tried to avoid him when he was in that condition. His wife, who was a simple and subservient woman, unfortunately received the brunt of his wrath by being beaten, which was a terrible scene to witness. The adults would try to appeal to him about this, when he was in a sensible condition, and he would invariably express regret, but the scenes were repeated. One time, we heard screams and saw Adam chasing his wife with the hatchet. Father decided to intervene. He chased after Adam, knocked him to the ground, disarmed him of the hatchet and told him that he never wanted to see anything like that again.

To make sure, Father informed him that from now on the hatchet would not stay in Adam's possession. In the mood he was in, Adam would have liked to kill Father but he knew that he could not best him. He lay on the ground as his rage and frustration slowly turned to sobbing. This encounter had a sobering effect on Adam and proved beneficial to our coexistence.

There was a certain amount of truth in my mother's accusation that Father lacked a sense of direction, especially when he was under stress. The first time Father went off alone, it was many hours after daybreak that he returned. We were frantic, of course, and certain that harm had come to him, and we begged Adam to go to look for him. He was reluctant to do so and assured us that Father was busy praying somewhere, or if he had lost his way, it would be good for him to find it on his own. As Adam finally agreed to set out to look for him, Father appeared, exhausted and distressed.

After making his 'social rounds' and receiving some handouts, he had left the gathering of potatoes until last. As he was busy filling his sack, a farmer noticed him in his field, gathering the potatoes. The farmer sneaked up on him with a knife and was ready to kill him, but Father swung the partially-filled sack and managed to land a lucky blow, which knocked the farmer out. Retrieving the knife and with all speed – though hampered by the weight of the food – Father took off for home. He reached the spot where he and Adam usually waited until dawn in order to identify their personalized markings, which would lead them to our site. The fear that he was being chased prevented him from allowing time to discern the markings. He became lost, and he had been wandering for hours before he finally found his way.

MORE FOREST LORE

Father's intervention and physical confrontation lowered Adam's stature a few pegs and set up the basis for a better relationship between the two men. Adam's attitude towards my brother and me became friendly. He began showing us things in the forest. For instance, to mark a trail, it was not enough to break a branch. The signs had to be in pairs, one mark not far from the other and in relation to a tree which had some outstanding features. There were mushrooms to be found and identified as edible, although it was already late in the season. He showed us how to prepare the fungus for starting a fire. How to avoid coming in contact with various strains of poison ivy, however, we learned through painful experience. A very important craft was how to make *postalee*. He half-heartedly showed us the process of obtaining and treating the strips of bark, but never taught us the intricacies of weaving them. It rained very heavily for several days and the spot where Adam had put up his hut became a virtual pool. By luck, ours was erected on higher ground and remained dry. Adam and his wife were forced to share our hut for two days and nights. When it stopped raining, we all pitched in, like pros, to erect a new hut. In appreciation, he made us each a pair of *postalee*. I tried many times to make a pair by copying the finished product but with questionable success.

The rains were coming more frequently and the colder, shorter days were signaling the approach of winter. We discovered spots in the hut that were leaking and we gathered more ferns to make it leak proof. As an additional precaution we used sharpened sticks to patiently dig a gully around the hut. To prevent the fire from being extinguished we put posts around it and made a detachable roof. The problem of food became more critical as the fields lay bare and every scrap of food had to be begged for. Carrying food in the cold and rainy nights was a great physical strain on my father.

It was Mother who first broached the issue of Grandmother's welfare. Mother insisted that under such conditions, Grandmother would not last the winter, and she advised Father to find a farmer – someone who could be trusted – to take her in. As she had done before, she could earn her keep by performing her medical services. There were also practical considerations, which Mother frankly stated. Such an arrangement would mean that there was one less mouth to feed, and there was also the possibility that the farmer who took her in would be a good source of food, when Father went to visit Grandmother. At first, Father objected to the idea and insisted that we must all stay together, but then he discussed it with Adam, who told him that Mother was right. He warned Father that it would be difficult enough to negotiate the snow empty-handed, let alone carrying any considerable load. One less mouth to feed would make a big difference. Grandmother accepted the idea, even if regretfully, as she understood that it was the only sensible thing for her to do.

Father went to the couple who had tended him in his state of amnesia and they willingly accepted Grandmother. It was very far away but Father was confident that they would take good care of her. It was a heart-rending scene, as Grandmother took out from her bag the little *sidur* (prayer book) which my Uncle Shmilke had hand-copied, and gave it to Father. We tearfully parted, and that was the last time that I saw my grandmother.

NO FUN IN WINTERLAND

Gradually it became very cold, especially at night. We did not have sufficient things with which to cover ourselves in order to retain our body heat. We did have our clothes, the little blanket, some rags and a lot of dried leaves and grass into which we burrowed ourselves, yet the below-freezing temperatures managed to cut through everything like a razor-sharp knife. Our teeth chattering, we spent many sleepless nights warming ourselves by the fire. Now there was a ghostly silence at dawn because of the absence of birds. When the sun appeared, I cheered it on as it melted the icicles which had formed on the trees like white beards. Then one day the sun did not appear and the snow began to fall. It was only last year that I had still thrilled at the sight of the first snow, chased the flakes with an open mouth and anticipated with delight the fun of winter activity. Now it seemed that each flake was landing straight on my heart, making it heavier with the burden of anticipation of the additional difficulties that winter would present.

The snow dictated new patterns of behavior. To begin with, it drastically limited our movements and, except for the purposes of bodily functions and restocking firewood, the days were spent in debilitating inactivity. Father and Adam got more than their share of strenuous activity in their frequent forays for food. The idea of washing our bodies verged on the suicidal and parasites began to take their toll. Mother tried in vain to wash one article of clothing at a time by pouring boiling water on it and then hanging it up to dry: it quickly became as stiff as a board and brittle with frost. We used our little soup pot to heat the water. Each piece of laundry had to be handled carefully because if it cracked, the material would tear. Our hair grew long, our bodies misshapen, with protruding stomachs, from lack of nutrition, and like apes we constantly scratched ourselves. If the skin between our toes was not washed and cleaned frequently enough, it cracked and a kind of fungus formed, which itched terribly and was painful. Yet we clung to our desire to live and to the hope that the Almighty would reward our struggle with redemption. The only thing which differentiated us from the apes, perhaps, was that my parents desperately held on to every vestige of humanity, which of course included our Judaism. Father recited his daily prayers; Shabbat and holidays were observed, as well as every other ritual that was part of our custom. One of the things which always amazed me – and to this day I do not know how she did it – was that Mother managed to maintain an exact Jewish calendar, including the days of minor holidays. On Shabbat we never fed the fire or cooked. We had no candles, of course, so Mother would set up two little piles of wood, and after she has removed the pot with food from the fire, she lit the little bonfires and recited the blessings over her two makeshift candles. Father would finish his evening prayers and we would sit down to eat our Shabbat meal. At first Father refused to make kiddush and say the blessing over the wine because we did not have any of the necessary articles to conduct the ceremony, and to make a blessing in vain was not allowed. Eventually he partly relented, at my mother's insistence, but skipped the blessing over the wine. We ate a little of the food, taking turns with our two-and-a-half spoons, and the rest was hung on a branch to be consumed on Shabbat. The first time we did that, even though the pot was covered with a rag, we discovered a drowned mouse in it. All we did was throw away the mouse. Rodents were interested in sharing our meager supply of food and we constantly had to devise techniques to prevent them from doing so. In the winter we devised a method of hanging the pot high enough above the fire to keep it tepid. As long as Adam was with us, he would disdainfully tend to our fire.

WE SET UP A COMMUNICATION SYSTEM

Although it happened less frequently now, Father had still sometimes to make his forays for food alone. He did not like Adam's system of reaching the spot where the trail markings began and waiting until dawn before following the trail. In the winter they had to resort to different markings because the forest assumed an entirely different aspect. After a new snowfall, the forest looked as if it was covered by a white sheet, under which many of the distinguishing landmarks disappeared. Footsteps in the snow could certainly not be depended upon because the wind or a new snowfall usually obliterated them. On the other hand, waiting was too dangerous because, alone and exhausted, Father could easily fall asleep and freeze to death. He taught us how to whistle very loudly, by placing two fingers in the mouth and blowing through them. In no time at all we mastered the craft, even to the point of imitating birdcalls. As was our custom, when Father was away, we baked and ate the thin layers of our allotted two potatoes each, and waited for the whistle. Sound travels very far on a cold night in the forest but sometimes it was a problem to pinpoint the direction. When Father became uncertain, he would whistle again to get his bearings, until we brought him safely home. It was a simple idea and no doubt it contributed to saving our lives.

THE ART OF BEGGING

Father learned that when you go begging for food, you cannot walk in with a bag indicating that you are already in possession of some, and definitely cannot walk in armed with a hatchet or a knife. He would stash away, in a safe place, whatever food he had accumulated, and enter each farmhouse empty-handed. There were times when, after he had surveyed his meager supply, he would spend hours at the potato storage hole in the fields, hacking away with the hatchet and the knife through the frozen ground and scooping away the dirt with his bare hands until he reached the potatoes. Then he would carefully cover them up again and hope that the wind and a new snowfall would cover his tracks.

One time, when Father was alone, just as he was about to enter a farmhouse, he was accosted by a number of young roughnecks. They were too many for him to put up a struggle and he decided to beg for mercy. The only mercy they showed was to drag him roughly to the local magistrate so that Father might be handed over to the Germans. The official knew and liked my father and told the Ukrainians to set him free. In fact, when Father told the story, he quoted the man as saying, 'I would give my life for Leiba.' Without having to be told twice, Father kissed the man's hands in gratitude and ran out of the house. Fearing that the men who brought him there might decide to take matters into their own hands – perhaps chase after him and kill him just to spite the magistrate – he retraced his steps and quickly hid in a stall with the horses. His assumption was correct, because a little while later he clearly heard, from his place of hiding, his captors take off in hot pursuit.

WHAT CAN OFFER GREATER COMFORT IN WINTER THAN A HORSE BLANKET?

It was in the stall that Father noticed a God-sent gift. One of the horses was covered, like a prince, with a large, heavy blanket. After waiting long enough to let his pursuers think that their prey had escaped, and go to sleep disappointed, Father folded the blanket, draped it around his neck and made his escape from the barn. When he retrieved his stashed-away food, he discovered that he was straining the limits of his strength by trying to carry both items. There was no option of leaving one of them behind or even of reducing the weight of the food by leaving some of it. He struggled with both until he reached the forest and then began a system of alternating between the two items. He would carry the food for a certain distance and then return for the blanket. It was a long, tedious and exhausting process and because of it, we suffered a good number of hours of anxiety until we finally heard the whistle. Mother went back with Father to help him carry the blanket the last few hundred meters. Never have I seen my father so exhausted, but he smiled happily and said to us: '*Es is do a groysser Gott, mayne tayere feigelach*' (God is great, my dear little birds). Only the following day did we receive a full account of what had transpired that terrible night. First he said his morning prayers and went to sleep demanding that he be awakened in time for Mincha and Maariv and then without even bothering to eat, he returned to the hut. That was the first night, since the beginning of winter, that we slept in warm comfort.

LIFE IS WORTH A BOTTLE OF VODKA

Whenever Father told the story of that event, he usually began by saying: 'My life is worth a bottle of vodka.' After our liberation, we made a special trip to see the man who saved Father's life, bearing some symbolic gifts – some bottles of *samagon*. The man looked at the bottles in appreciation and then laughed and filled us in on the events that had followed. It seems that the men who captured Father were very unhappy with the magistrate's verdict and, being foiled in their attempt to recapture him, decided to inform the chief of the Ukrainian police. The latter did not deem the issue lightly and gave the magistrate two days to deliver Leiba. If that did not happen, he would inform the Germans. The next day, the magistrate took a bottle of *samagon* to the policeman's house, and by the time they had finished the bottle, the matter was forgotten. Looking at the two bottles and then at us, the man remarked that he certainly had made a good deal.

HELP IS ON THE WAY BUT ADAM AND HIS WIFE LEAVE US

News began to filter through that the Russians had stopped the German advance and were, in fact, on the offensive. To help in the war effort, Russian officers had arrived to organize the Partisans as an effective fighting force. The immediate result of strengthening the Partisans and uniting them under a central command was a reduction in the numbers and the effectiveness of the Bulbovtsi. In the spring, Adam found out that his son, who had been sent by Russians into the area to help organize the Partisans, was looking for him. It took a while but eventually contact was established between them.

Adam's son was able to bring his parents to the Partisans but had no influence in allowing us to join them. All of us accompanied Adam and his wife part of the way, because Father had decided that this was a good opportunity to move our location closer to civilization. At a certain point, Father told us that we had reached the area where we were to set up our new site. Adam approved of the choice and both men laughed and embraced each other. We had been together for more than eight months, and although there had been occasional strife, the common experience and hardships had cemented into a strong friendship. Adam and his wife left us whatever they felt they could spare, or could replace with the help of the Partisans. As a gesture of his true friendship and love, Adam gave Father his *smekalka*. They took off, never to be seen again, and we set to work on building a new hut.

Twice during the winter, Father made the long trip to visit Grandmother. She was lonely and missed us terribly, but under the circumstances, that was a small price to pay for her comparative comfort and security. Father comforted her as well as he could and promised her that during the summer he would bring her to stay with us for a while. Because of the distance, we knew that Father would be away for two nights. The generosity of the people who tended to Grandmother was overwhelming, and he returned from those visits laden with staples. On one occasion he even brought salted pork. My brother and I were already veterans at eating this meat but my parents had avoided it for as long as possible. Now Father declared that it was a question of *'piku'ach nefesh'* (saving a life) and both of them remorsefully joined us. I can still see the pained expression on their faces and that look is one of the reasons that I refrain from touching that meat to this day.

GRANDMOTHER'S SERVICES WERE NEEDED ELSEWHERE

Now that it was summer and we were much closer to where grandmother was staying, Father decided that it was time to fulfill his promise to her. But when he arrived, the couple regretfully informed him that his mother had passed away about a month ago. There had been a typhoid epidemic in the area, and while trying to treat patients with this fatal and infectious disease, she had contracted it herself. We all joined in Father's grief; we sat with him during shiva (seven days of mourning) and comforted and reassured him when he began to blame himself for agreeing to leave Grandmother with the farmer. He could not even recite the Kaddish, because according to Jewish practice, ten males over the age of 13 are needed for that prayer.

'Man is stronger than a stone', states an old Yiddish expression and no doubt, considering our miserable existence, with only a faint hope of survival, the statement certainly applied to us. To say that 'man adjusts to suffering' is ridiculous. Man never becomes immune to the excruciating pain of loss, the debilitating effect of fear or the nagging realization of uncertainty. At best, if he is strong enough mentally and physically, he manages to endure. That is what we did. Mentally we clung to hope, and physically – luckily and unexplainably –

none of us became seriously ill, during the entire period. Before the war, despite his physical strength, Father had suffered from chronic asthma. The slightest cold or change of season would cause him terrible discomfort. He would be plagued by terrible attacks and traveled to see doctors from whom he received all kinds of medication, but the only thing that really helped him was Grandmother's treatment. She would fill a pot with water and some herbs, boil them, place a towel over Father's head and make him inhale the escaping steam. Father would reappear red as a lobster from this treatment but would begin breathing with greater ease. What caused his miraculous recovery we never knew, but not once during our stay in the forest did his asthma occur again. He laughingly claimed that it was the Ukrainians and the Germans who knocked it out of him.

ADAPTING TO LIFE WITHOUT ADAM

The fact that we had accumulated some knowledge and experience in the art of survival in the forest did not diminish the dangers, dilemmas and near calamities that still lay ahead of us. Since we were closer to civilization, we began the practice of changing locations more frequently, especially during the warmer months. Sometimes we would be accidentally discovered by a farmer herding his cattle, or the mosquitoes in a particular location were unbearable, or Father felt that he had exhausted the generosity and patience of the surrounding farmers. Whenever we reached a new site, the first thing we checked for was the availability of the basic requirements of water, enough fallen trees for firewood, and saplings and ferns. My brother and I would continue to scout the area, if it was a new neighborhood, and return with mushrooms, berries and detailed descriptions of what we had seen. Of particular importance and interest to us was to see if we could locate the tracks of larger animals. It was not advisable to move into an area which a pack of wolves had made their territory.

THE SCOUTS ARE BEING SCOUTED

On one occasion, when we were scouting a new area, we realized that we were being followed by something. It was not a human being because whenever we stopped to make markings, the rustling continued for a few extra seconds. Adam had pointed out to us that when a human follows his prey, he stops almost as instantly as his prey, whereas animals react a little more slowly. Although we were very scared we did not dare to turn around, until some instinct told us that our follower was too close for comfort, and then we both turned and screamed. Our screaming began for the purpose of frightening whatever was following us, but it continued from terror as we saw a wolf come to a halt about five meters away from us. The wolf turned and ran as we continued our screaming and whistling, which quickly brought Father to our aid. We decided not to camp there, of course, on the assumption that this had not been a lone wolf.

During one of our forays to reconnoiter our new location, we noticed a very big bird leave her nest as we approached her tree. What seemed strange was that the bird did not fly off, but continued to circle around us and emit all kinds of noises. Unfamiliar as I am with bird talk, I would suggest that the bird was saying, 'Keep away from my nest, you nasty brats.' As our curiosity was aroused, however, we continued to investigate and discovered the nest. The bird became really frantic when we found about four or five relatively large eggs. For us this was a treasure of food. We took the eggs and returned to our campsite, with the bird still circling around us. We showed our treasure to Mother and when she heard the poor bird's frantic chirping, she said to us, 'Return the eggs to where you found them!' When we began to protest, she took two eggs and said, 'You see these two eggs: they're the two of you', and then pointed at the bird: 'That's me. If anyone tried to hurt you, I would also become frantic.' There was no need for further explanations. As quickly and as gently as possible we returned the eggs. We did not develop a lasting, cordial relationship with the bird but the incident did teach us to appreciate and respect the wildlife around us. We already respected the wolf, of course, from as far away as possible.

MY BROTHER IS LOST

Another near calamity had to do with my brother, and it was under similar circumstances, when we were scouting an area. For some reason he was alone: most likely I was too scared, after the last incident, to join him. He had no intention of wandering off too far, but for the first time he came practically face to face with a big boar. Although the animal did not do anything, the sight of it caused my brother to panic and, abandoning all the rules of safety, he followed his first instinct and ran. Unfortunately, he ran in the wrong direction and for too great a distance, until he realized that nothing was chasing him. When he tried to make his way back, he discovered that he was lost. Being lost in the woods was not a new experience for him and he tried to stay calm. He thought he heard whistling and shouting but he was not certain of the direction from which it came. He did not answer for fear of attracting the beast, and tried in vain to find his way back, until he was completely exhausted. He decided to rest a little and fell asleep. In the meantime, when we became aware that my brother had not returned, we began to look for him. It did not take long before the three of us became frantic, and setting aside all caution, we called out my brother's name and whistled: 'Pinja! Pinja! Pinchas! Pinchas!' The woods were reverberating with the sound of his name and my shrill whistle. It was late in the day; it was cold and cloudy and it began to rain. We knew that he was not wearing anything warm and would most certainly freeze to death in the approaching night. When we were certain that there was no chance of finding him, because there was no response to our calling or even to my shrill whistling – which had become a form of communication between us – we reached the point of hysterically mourning the loss of my brother. Suddenly we heard his whistle. Within a very short time we were reunited. The amazing part of this incident, which my brother told us, was that while he was sleeping, our two grandmothers came to him in his dream, woke him up, insisted that he should start to whistle, and he had followed their instructions.

Winter was approaching and we knew from experience the additional hardships which that season presented. Had we known at the time that there was still another winter in the forest, ahead of us we might have given in to Mother's occasional pleading to give ourselves up and put an end to our suffering. Hope and belief that the Almighty was somehow guiding our path, however, and bits of news about the Russian advance, strengthened our resolve to survive.

During the warm months we walked barefoot but when it became necessary to wear shoes, my father and brother were unfortunate. Father's shoes were in a dilapidated state because of much use and were tied up with strings and rags. Accidentally he discovered that the increase made to the size of his foot by the addition of the rags made his footsteps sink less deeply into the snow – makeshift snow shoes! On the other hand, the rags increased the amount of snow that stuck on and when they became wet and then froze, he would be dragging blocks of ice. When he returned, Mother would carefully pour on cold water to thaw the rags and we could see that in some places they were actually frozen to his foot. My brother simply outgrew his shoes, which made it very painful for him to wear them. I tried to make him *postelee* but they were nowhere near to the quality, of those which Adam made, and they would quickly fall apart. Yet somehow we made it through another winter.

THE BENEFITS OF PRIVATE ENTERPRISE

By the summer of 1943, news of Russian success on the front was more encouraging. The Partisans' contribution became more effective by paralyzing German supply lines and they in turn became more ruthless with the Ukrainians. The Bulbovtsi were practically obliterated by the Partisans and as a result the general attitude, even of the formerly hostile Ukrainians, became friendlier. The most exciting news, as we finally discovered, was that the Americans had joined the war. We began to stay closer to civilization, partly because of the friendlier atmosphere and maybe because of the fatalistic attitude which we had developed. In fact there were occasions when we all set out together in search of food.

The effect of all this was that when the farmers looked at me and my brother, their hearts were invariably softened when they also heard my parents relate our ordeal of the past year and a half. Mother, who was a very practical woman, reached a very practical arrangement during her conversations with the women. She offered her services to knit sweaters. This new arrangement had a number of positive effects. We were not viewed as beggars but as entrepreneurs who had come to make a deal, take measurements and in the process conduct an amicable conversation. The farmers provided the wool; we easily shaped wooden needles; and this became a rewarding enterprise, to which I also made my contribution by learning how to knit. This was the first time that we had received food in return for our labor, although we never argued over the amount of remuneration.

One night, as we were returning to our campsite from one of our visits to farmers in the area, we heard the sharp clicks of rifle bolts and the order: '*Stoy!*' (halt). My brother and I screamed, expecting a bullet in the next instant, but Father yelled, '*Svayee!*' (one of us). Shots did not follow, because this was a Partisan scouting party. They were not exactly friendly, but luckily there was a Jewish man in the group who intervened on our behalf. They did not intend to harm us but they were angry with my parents for hiding out like mice, instead of joining the Partisans and fighting. Father explained that he would gladly do so but pointed at us and told them that no one would accept us. They replied that if he showed his worth by obtaining two rifles, we could all join them. Such a request was like asking Father to turn the forest into a lake. We parted, with an admonition to Father that he had better obtain those rifles: otherwise, in our next encounter, we would not be so lucky.

OUR STINT WITH THE PARTISANS

We did not join the Partisans but they joined us. As we approached the area where our campsite was, we discovered that hundreds of people had invaded our domain. We were certain that they were Partisans, but after our previous encounter with them the other night, we decided that it was the better part of valor to avoid them. It was inevitable that they would eventually discover our campsite because it was close to where they were. When they found us the next day, the reception was contrary to what we had feared. We were not driven off or harassed but in fact they befriended us, and even if we could not join them officially, we were awarded the status of welcome camp followers. It was a very large group and some of the more considerate amongst them brought us food and spent time talking to my parents. One man brought us a colorful tin can decorated with the intertwined Russian and American flags. We had no idea what it was but the man explained as he opened it that this was food sent from America. The concept, for me, was amazing – that such a thing was possible – and even more exciting was the news that Russia was not the only country fighting the Germans: that the Americans and other nations were maintaining fronts of their own against them.

We found out that a party had just returned from a mission to mine a supply road which the Germans frequently used. The operation was successful, from the reports of those who had carried it out. There was a Jewish man in the party who gleefully told us that he heard the wounded Germans screaming: *'Lieber Gott, was machst Du mit uns?'* (Dear God, what are

138

you doing to us?) To hear that Germans were dying was good news for us. Several days later, a German reprisal came in the form of a massive air attack. It did not last very long but it was devastating, with many Partisans killed or injured. Quickly, the dead were buried, the injured were treated, and the Partisans broke camp and began to move on.

The leader denied Father's request that we should be allowed to go with them, or at least be given a rifle, but he agreed to leave Father a pair of boots, which were removed from one of the casualties. This was the end of our short role as Partisans. The assumption that the Germans would be satisfied with the bombing alone proved wrong. It had been only a softening-up operation. Later in the day we heard noises and the barking of dogs and we knew that it was not the Partisans returning. We began running deeper into the woods but it seemed that this time we were trapped, as we clearly heard the shouting of orders and the excited barking of dogs. We came across a big crater (caused by a bomb which had landed way off the mark) which was already partially filled with water, and we crawled into it. It would be a matter of minutes before the dogs discovered us, and so we tearfully began to make our farewells and to hug each other. I stoutly but tearfully maintained – not from false hope nor as mindless words of comfort – that this was not the end. I said: 'We will someday be in Eretz Yisroel.' The minutes passed and the dogs must have lost our scent, because of the terrible aroma of sulfur left behind by exploding bombs in the section of marsh in which we were hiding. The Germans, realizing that the Partisans had retreated and dispersed in different directions, decided quickly to vacate the area. It was not to their advantage to be caught in a surprise attack by Partisans in the forest. Invariably when it did happen they would suffer severe casualties. Soon silence invaded the forest, for even the birds fled the area during the upheaval. We had escaped another brush with untimely death and I received another chance to fulfill my promise to live in Israel.

OUR TRIBUTE TO HUMANITY AND JUDAISM HELPS TO PRESERVE US

The holidays were particularly difficult to bear. Even if I did not fully grasp the cultural and social significance of observing holidays, I was aware of their religious content. They were made particularly difficult to bear by tender memories of the same festive occasions being spent in the company of loved ones. Except for my parents and my brother, my loved ones were all dead. Hunted and insignificant as we were in the eyes of our pursuers, plagued by fear and uncertainty of the coming day, we still managed to offer expressions of observance on these occasions. It was a testament to our determination to survive and provide credence to our humanity and Judaism. It was an act of love to our God and defiance to our oppressors.

How well I remember this particular incident of Yom Kippur in 1943. We were in a new location, dwarfed by gigantic trees. Father turned towards them and with a choked voice, and tears in his eyes, ironically invited the trees to join him in the minyan, as he sang Kol Nidre and recited the rest of Maariv by heart. Mother added, in the same vein, that since we had so much experience of fasting, it would not be a hardship now. As was the usual case on these occasions, the futility of our plight and the desperate state of our existence evoked bitter tears. Mother, who was particularly disheartened by our condition and suffered most from our ordeal, primarily because it was difficult for her to helplessly observe the miserable state of her children, again advocated that we should put an end to our suffering and give ourselves up. This plea was not new to my father, my brother and me, of course, but we opposed the idea by pointing out that we had managed to survive thus far against all odds and we could not give up now. Each expression of hope put forward, by one of the three of us increased the emotionally-charged atmosphere, so that we all ended up crying bitterly, our tears a mixture of hope and desperation. Father strengthened our determination by reciting some passages from the Psalms and reaffirming his trust in the Almighty with a few well-chosen words in Yiddish. Thus comforted and motivated by hope and a desire to live, we continued our struggle until the next crisis.

TREES TO THE RESCUE

The trees, which could not participate in the minyan, took an active part in saving our lives. We maintained a constant fire, to keep warm and to discourage wolves and boars from approaching us. A German plane spotted the fire. Assuming that this was a Partisan camp, the pilot dropped eight bombs all around us – we counted the craters. Looking at the carnage next morning, we were certain that the trees had saved our lives by deflecting the bombs and taking the brunt of the punishment. It was an amazing sight to see the trees form a kind of protective umbrella over the hut in which we slept. Had any one of those big branches, hanging above us, detached itself, it would have crushed us to death. It was as if these trees sacrificed themselves for our sake. The four of us came out of this incident shaken up but unscratched. The stench of sulfur and devastation forced us to move to another place.

One day, a man who served as a kind of forest ranger came across our site. It turned out to be the same man, who years ago had met my father sitting in the middle of the road, on the verge of giving himself up, and dissuaded him from doing it. The reunion was so beautifully human and heart-warming and my father expressed his gratitude for the man's sensible advice. The man's generosity was singular because he told us that he had a house in the forest and invited us to come and stay with him. We gladly accepted the invitation and pitched in to help, with much energy and long hours, with all the chores around the house and with increasing the clearing of land that he used for farming. The man was happy with our company and our contribution. One early morning, as Father

141

and the man were sawing logs, Father noticed some human forms surreptitiously trying to approach the house. Instinctively, Father yelled for us to come out, and advised the man that he and his family should join us, but he refused to listen. We ran for the closest point of the woods as bullets whistled by us. Before we reached the safety of the trees, my brother caught a bullet in the calf of his leg. Father noticed him fall, picked him up and continued running. A little later we heard some more shots and then saw thick smoke rise above the trees: it was obvious what that meant. There was not much time to contemplate the tragedy of the people who had treated us so kindly, because then we saw blood on my father's clothes, and my brother began to complain about a pain in his leg. It was a flesh wound, but the bleeding had to be stopped and the wound cleaned and bandaged. Some sixth sense had made us leave most of our meager belongings inside the hut at our last site, and camouflage it. The reason behind this was, primarily, not to give our generous host the impression that we were moving in with him, but only coming for a short visit. We found the site, which was not too far away, the way we had left it, and Mother immediately began to treat my brother's wound. She stopped the bleeding; cleaned it constantly; applied certain leaves and bandages; and although the area of the wound was swollen for a while, within a comparatively short time it healed. My brother was left with a permanent souvenir on his leg.

Although the Nazi killing machine had familiarized me with such beastly and mindless murder, it was difficult for me to erase from my mind the faces of the kind forest ranger and his family. Somehow the Germans missed killing the family's huge but gentle dog. I think that he joined us when he saw us running to the woods and then returned later when he realized we were not playing a game with him. The dog must have realized what had happened to his master and the family. Many days and nights afterwards we heard the poor animal howling and bemoaning his master. There was nothing that we could do for him except cry as well. Finally the baying stopped.

WINTER IS AGAIN AT THE DOORSTEP

There was another winter approaching, and although we were seasoned veterans of the hardships it presented, we were scared. There were a number of things working in our favor, however: we stayed as close as possible to civilization; our sweater-making business was in demand; and the Germans retreated faster during the harsh winters. We were certain that if we managed to survive this one, we would be liberated. Stories of the Russian gains and Partisan accomplishments may have been exaggerated, because we had been hearing about them for a long time. In any outright confrontation, the superior forces of the Germans had the upper hand, leaving countless bodies of Partisans to be consumed by wolves. The Partisans' primary effectiveness lay in their ability to ambush convoys, and railways and to mine roads. As time went on, the confidence of the Partisans had increased, as well as their numbers, and we would hear them singing military Russian songs at night as they moved about. In rural areas, the Partisans began to gain control but would retreat to the forest when they learned of the advance of large German columns. In the winter the Germans would avoid undertaking such missions. While making our way to deliver two sweaters, we came upon a wide path in the forest, solidly packed down in the snow. Its condition indicated that many men had traveled it.

Naturally we assumed that a large Partisan group had made it. When we delivered the sweaters we discovered that it had been created by an advance Russian army force which had then unfortunately retreated. It was strange that we had not heard any shooting or explosions, but it was explained to us, that the actual front was still hundreds of kilometers away. The intricacies of military strategy were a mystery to us and although we were comforted by the signs of Russian success, we were disappointed that we had not known of the advance group, because perhaps we would have followed them when they retreated. This was a most unlikely possibility but a comforting thought.

PASSOVER SAVES THE DAY

Despite our dire circumstances, on Pesach (Passover) we would not eat bread. We would even go through the ritual of making the dishes kosher for Pesach and Father would conduct the ceremony of *bedikat* chametz. We would hoard whatever was possible for the eight days of Pesach, so that during that period Father would not go out to search for food and face the dilemma of having to refuse bread, because he could hardly accept it and throw it away later. Long before Pesach he would begin to beg for and occasionally receive some flour that was made of buckwheat. We saved that flour carefully and during Pesach we used it to make something which resembled a matza. These days, when we were making sweaters and the farmers were becoming more generous, we could state our preferences for food and managed to accumulate a considerable quantity of buckwheat flour, as Pesach was approaching.

There was no mistaking that the dull, distant thuds were battle explosions. As time progressed they became louder. Previously the Germans had avoided rural areas, but now they occupied any territory from which they could halt the Russian advance – and that was very slow going. One day we discovered that the Germans were sharing our part of the woods with us. That is, they were located on a road leading through the forest called the Shlach. This road was reportedly constructed by Napoleon during his retreat. There was no question of our going out in search of food or of maintaining a fire. We finished whatever available food we had and then, for about a week, our nutrition consisted of the flour, which we had saved for Pesach, diluted in water. Luckily the Germans departed before we finished all the flour prepared in this manner, because the paste would have finished us. It was a little while after Pesach, in the spring of 1944, that we met our liberators, a group of Russian soldiers. We had survived!

4 It is Hard to be Free

To describe in words the sensation of being free, after all these years of oppression and being hunted, is an impossible task. Not that I lack the words to describe it, or that the many years that have passed since then have dulled my memory of that particular moment, but because no matter how eloquently, succinctly or elaborately I phrase it, the actual sensation cannot be conveyed. Furthermore, the idea that I was free took a long time to penetrate my mind, and for me to become adjusted to it. It did not seem natural to encounter a strange person and not be suspicious of his intentions; to hear a loud noise and not suspect that you were being shot at and must search for shelter; to hear people arguing and realise that they are not actually angry with you. On the occasions when I relaxed alone, immersed in my own thoughts, oblivious to events around me, I would wake up with a start to the wonderful sensation of being free and the happiness of being alive.

Once we overcame the euphoria of being liberated and the reality of our new situation dawned upon us, the question arose: 'What course to follow next?' Since we began our terrible odyssey of suffering when we left Kortiless, we decided that we would begin our newly-found freedom there. The bitter reality that we found there drove home with full force the futility of our future. Again we realized, as we had almost three years before, while we were hiding in the cornfield next to my grandparents' house, that we could never again consider Kortiless to be our home. From this village, we were the only four Jews who had survived. Although we were glad to be alive – a privilege for which we had suffered severely – we could not help but wonder why God had chosen us to deserve life. As we surveyed the ruins of what was once our home, the homes of our loved ones and the rest of the Jewish community, the joy of life abandoned us. In brief, the essence of our lives lay in ruins.

WHAT IS THE REALITY OF OUR LIFE?

Mother understood that the purpose of our survival was to remember all those who had died. Consequently, in the ensuing years, memorial candles were constantly burning in my parents' home. Father continued to relate, with precise details and great stress on the role of the Almighty, the saga of our survival. He would always remember to add, 'There were so many people I knew who were worthier than me, yet for some reason here I am.' I rarely discussed the after-effects of our experience with my brother, but my impression is that he developed a philosophical and intellectual attitude. He attributes our ability to cope with the situation to the strength and determination of the human spirit to survive. I chose to suppress everything all these years. I felt that my human dignity had suffered most from this ordeal, and that made it so difficult for me to speak about it. I find it very hard to listen to the self-styled messengers of survival: people who claim that they have been spared by divine intervention, in order that they may tell the world the events that transpired. To my mind, this kind of person establishes for himself a delusion of preferential treatment and a claim that his story is unique because of the element of providence. I am certainly glad that the person survived, and it is his prerogative to believe what he wants, but he should not try to advance this kind of trivial theory to other survivors. There were just as many unique stories as there were survivors.

Although there were many Ukrainian casualties in the village and most of the homes were burned, we noticed that new ones were being put up, including the beginning of a new *tserkva* (church). We knew that the synagogue would never rise from its ashes, and history would never tell us that it once stood on that spot. We met some of our former neighbors and others in the village, who looked at us as if we were ghosts and expressed their amazement that we had survived. Very properly they showed their sympathy, by shedding crocodile tears for those Jews who had died. Most of these people were two-faced and never lifted a finger to aid those victims whom they now so expertly bewailed. On the contrary, they had aided our tormentors and we hated them for it. Father inquired if anyone had heard of the whereabouts of Kolya, but no one, including his own father, knew anything. Although my father was a gentle person, there is no doubt that he personally would have extracted a terrible vengeance upon that man.

BACK TO RATNO

Since the beginning of the diaspora, Jews have tried to stay together, and therefore we returned to Ratno, in the hope that we would find some survivors there. I will spare the details of what we looked like when we arrived in that little city. We did find some Jews, but not even enough to form an official minyan (ten males). They looked at us and they did understand the reason for our miserable condition because their lot was no easier. There was no problem in finding shelter in one of the many abandoned Jewish homes, whose former owners would never return to reclaim them and which were not occupied as yet by the local *Myestchani* (Ukrainian city dwellers). The problem of food was critical but somehow Father managed either to earn or to borrow some rubles and with them we obtained the essential ingredients for baking bread. Mother also baked an item called *bublitchki* (rolls). My brother and I sold the rolls and some of the bread, primarily to Russian soldiers. They gladly purchased them and eagerly asked if we also happened to have any *samagon*. When we conveyed this demand to Father, he quickly realized the potential of such an item with the thirsty Russian soldiers.

MAKING HOME-BREWED VODKA

With a little money and some empty bottles, the four of us set out once again, in the direction of Kortiless. Father located a farmer who had a still; purchased potatoes from him for a fair price; and made a brew, very similar to vodka, called *samagon*. We then returned to Ratno and quickly disposed of the brew at a fine profit. Father made at least two more trips alone and repeated the process of making the liquor, but then told us that it was too dangerous to go back to Kortiless now because the Bulbovtsi had become active again in rural areas.

FATHER BECOMES A COMMISSAR AND A PROSPECTIVE SOLDIER

Because he knew how to read and write Russian, Father became an official in the temporary administration that was set up. The war was still going on and able-bodied men were constantly conscripted into the army in the most beastly manner. One day, without any warning, Father was accosted in the street by an officer and some soldiers, and ordered to fall in with the rest of the men they had recruited. There was nothing that he could do. No explanation or reasoning was accepted, and the fact that he was an official was apparently even more reason why he should be prepared to fight for the motherland. All the conscripts were imprisoned at a military base in town, where they waited to be marched off to an induction centre in another city. Father somehow managed to get word to Mother of his predicament.

Once again, Mother became the force that guided our family. It was she who had to make the decisions and take the necessary steps to secure Father's release. She was determined and certain that there must be a way to bring that about. At first she tried at a local level and even got as far as the commanding officer. The most she accomplished, however, was to obtain the officer's sympathy, with her tale of the ordeals of the forest, the fact that we had been with the Partisans, and that without Father, at this point, we would be lost. The officer remained adamant. He must bring all his recruits to the induction centre in the city of Ludsk. If the doctors there, however, could proclaim Father unfit for medical reasons he would be released.

A few days later, a column of about a hundred men and one woman – my mother – set out on foot towards the city of Ludsk. She made arrangements with some people to keep an eye on us and left us explicit instructions how to take care of ourselves. We watched helplessly as Father was marched off. Walking at the side, because she was not allowed to join the column, was Mother. She had no idea how she was going to bring about Father's release, but it was certain that she would stop at nothing and would face all hardships.

MY BROTHER AND I HATCH OUR OWN ADVENTURES

It was summer, there was no school, and my brother and I had no friends, because there were no other Jewish or Christian children in the vicinity with whom we could play. We wandered around town, trying to pass away the time. Occasionally we did find Ukrainian playmates, but these encounters were usually brief. Invariably we became easy targets upon whom they tried to assert their superiority and authority. This did not usually sit well with my brother and me. One day we noticed some Russian soldiers who were trying to fix a truck. Observing this activity offered a marvelous opportunity to pass away the time. We discovered that the soldiers were heading for the city of Kovel, about fifty kilometers away. My family and I had been to Kovel since our liberation and had met some of the Jewish people there who survived. Because it had a larger Jewish population to begin with, proportionally more Jews survived in Kovel. Father was finally able to pray in a minyan there, even if he had to coerce some of the men to join him. The services took place in the remains of the large synagogue that was at one time, we were told, very beautiful. There was no sign of the doors, windows, benches, *bimah*, the ark or even the floor. Only the walls were left and they told, literally, a very sad story. The Nazis had packed hundreds of Jews into the synagogue for many days before finally executing them. The unfortunate people wrote and scratched desperate messages on every available space on the walls. The contents were heart-rending, including appeals to remember them, and cries for revenge. Here Father, with his beautiful voice, had conducted the service and finally had his chance of reciting Kaddish. After the brief service was over, most of the people silently sat down on the floor and wept. The reason we had not, as yet, moved to Kovel was because most of the Jews we spoke to did not intend to remain there, and except for expressing the dream of going to Eretz Yisroel, no one had a clear idea of what they were going to do. In the meantime, we had returned to Ratno because Father had employment there.

When the roar of the motor sounded and the Russian truck began to move, it had two additional passengers: my brother and I. On the spur of the moment and with the tacit approval of the soldiers, my brother decided that we were going to Kovel. Fifty kilometers is a relatively short distance to cover in a vehicle, but because of the frequent breakdowns, we did not reach our destination until the next morning. We found some people who took care of us. We told them our woes, about Father being conscripted and Mother accompanying him in an effort to have him released. They sympathized with our misfortune and did not consider our actions terrible but they advised us against continuing towards Ludsk and urged us instead to return to Ratno. Their argument was that if Mother was unsuccessful in her efforts to secure Father's release, Ratno is where she would return, and not finding us there would be disastrous for her. After several days, provided with some food, we set out early in the morning, on our return trip.

At first we hoped that some army vehicle would pass by, but after wasting a good part of the morning in vain, and still fifty kilometers away, we started to walk.

It was nearing sunset and we were only about halfway home. Since we considered ourselves free, we did not think twice about approaching a house, in a little village we came across, and requesting to be put up for the night. We told them the sad tale of our father being abducted into the Russian army and Mother's efforts to release him. We explained that the reason we were on the road was because we had tried to look for them. Our story produced a good response and we were welcomed. The mistake we made was in assuming that the leopard had changed its spots: we then told them that we were Jewish. We realized our mistake by the sudden silence that followed and an abrupt end to the friendly atmosphere. We were taken to sleep in a barn. A little later, my brother had to urinate and when he went outside, a boy about his age met him. Children do not hide their feelings. The boy began by abusing my brother verbally, with well-known phrases, and then tried to strike him. My brother managed to ward him off but the boy continued with his verbal abuse, adding that tonight he would enjoy watching us suffer when the adults got hold of us. I was asleep when my brother returned; he roughly woke me up and told me that we must escape immediately. I will never know if there was any truth to the boy's threats about the adults' intentions, but we preferred to take our chances with the wolves. We must have made the remainder of the journey in record time because it was still dark when we reached our empty home in Ratno.

MOTHER'S DETERMINATION CUTS SHORT MY FATHER'S MILITARY CAREER

Mother knew that her only hope of releasing Father from the army was a doctor's verdict that he was not fit. The first thing she did was to find a Jewish family with whom she could stay.

151

When she explained the reason for her presence in Ludsk, her hosts became busy and, with the help of others, quickly discovered that one of the examining doctors was Jewish. A meeting was arranged and Mother begged him to intervene, once again relating our saga of suffering and saying that for father to be sent off to the war at this point was simply unjust. The doctor explained that it was very difficult to obtain a medical release from the army and that such a thing was issued only with the approval of a committee of three doctors. When she told the doctor that Father used to suffer terribly from asthma attacks, he promised to examine him and see what could be done. During Father's conversation with the doctor, he was asked if he was allergic to anything or whether he remembered what used to bring on the asthma attacks. The only thing that Father could tell the doctor was that he did not like onions. The doctor decided that it was worth a try and told Mother to deliver a generous amount of onions and make Father eat them. It worked: Father became pitifully sick. In that condition the doctor brought him before the committee, where he explained that he had never met with a case like this and strongly advised that Father be released, for fear that his condition might be contagious. The committee very wisely approved Father's release, for the safety of the Red Army. He obtained a certificate, confirmed by three doctors, declaring that his health was in such a poor state that he could not serve the motherland as a warrior, but should return, post-haste, to his administrative duties in Ratno. It was not certain whether he had a recurrence of his asthma attacks but, according to Father, he had consumed so many onions that they would have made anyone sick. He wheezed and coughed and was short of breath for several days after he was released. Mother was afraid that maybe some real damage had been caused, but even before Father had completely recuperated they began their journey home.

To this day, when things happen to me that are beyond my expectations and make me indescribably happy, I call them a gift from God. In spite of the fact that I am not a religious man anymore and do not feel worthy of divine intervention, I viewed my father's return as a gift from God, regardless of Mother's considerable contribution to this miracle. Father, who never wavered in his faith in the Almighty, offered Mother her due by reaffirming his belief in divine providence, but added that it had also required Mother's courage in following the opportunity which He had provided.

When my parents heard of our thoughtless expedition to Kovel, they were aghast, and for the first time we were properly scolded, although my brother received the brunt of it. This incident, however, spurred on a discussion regarding our future. It was clear that we would not stay in Ratno, but as long as the war continued there was no other choice. We were afraid of moving to a larger city because of the problem of earning a living, and had no desire to move deeper into Russia as some other survivors did. Our decision was that when the war was over, we would follow our dream of reaching Eretz Yisroel, but in the meantime we had to make the best of our difficult situation.

SETTLING DOWN TO THE REALITY OF LIFE

In the meantime, my brother and I were enrolled into school, which for various reasons began after a delay of about three months. For me, this was a new experience and it was a terrible one. I had dreamed of going to school one day in Kortiless, while my uncle was still the principal. Now, three years overdue, I began my dream under dreadful conditions. There were many children from the ages of 6 to 16, who were gathered into one room. It took several days before we actually began our academic pursuits, which proved less than adequate. During that time we were subjected to boring and repetitive speeches, by various functionaries and teachers, about the glory of Stalin and Lenin and the victorious forces of Mother Russia, who were on the verge of annihilating Nazi Germany and its leader. We cheerfully joined in with these declarations shouting 'Hurrah' three times when the signal was given. Finally, classes were formed and I found myself in grade one. I achieved this status by honestly answering, 'No' to all the questions that I was asked about my academic achievements, aside from the cheder which in their eyes did not exist and did not amount to anything.

The didactic requirements upon the teachers were not overly strenuous and the curriculum was such that it did not place any undue stress on their abilities. It consisted of learning to read and write and to do arithmetic. Anyone who was beyond that level was essentially considered a graduate, although there were still the post graduate activities of accumulating a repertoire of Russian songs, learning nationalistic poems by heart and undergoing consistent indoctrination sessions. School supplies could not be obtained but each pupil was given a notebook, a pencil and a big eraser. There was no such thing as blank paper to be purchased in Ratno. The teacher began the lesson by writing on the blackboard the name of our glorious father, Stalin, and eventually we had to copy that into our notebooks. First we had to practice, and that was done in another notebook, made up of newspaper pages, with a pencil that had to be constantly wetted with the tongue so that our writing would show up above the print. When we reached a level of perfection which satisfied the teacher, we could then copy it into our clean notebook, under her supervision. My knowledge of the Cyrillic alphabet, which Tanya had taught me, quickly returned to me. While the rest of the students were still struggling with each letter, the tips of their tongues blue from the constant wetting of pencils, I managed to copy the entire name on the newspaper and was ready to write it in my notebook: Yosef Viseryonovitch Stalin.

The teacher moved around the classroom encouraging each student with '*Charasho*' (nice) and '*Molodyets*' (exemplary), and as she approached me I expected that the praises would be overwhelming. She looked at my accomplishment and remained silent, for what seemed to me an exceedingly long time. She was looking for the right words, but they were not praise. In a loud voice she called me '*Durak*' (stupid), then turned towards the class and asked: 'Why is it that Jews always have to prove how clever they are, and why do they always have to lie?' Although she did not use the pejorative word *Szydi*, but the accepted *Yivreyee*, the prejudicial anti-Semitic message was the same. My rebbe's ear-twisting was like a love pat in comparison, because then the pain was physical, but in this case my dignity was being undermined and as I sat frozen to the spot, a bitter heaviness settled over my body. My face turned red from anger and shame, not from the insult but because I was remaining silent. The last time I had heard an anti-Semitic remark I was helpless and insignificant, but now I was a free person, yet I remained speechless and thus betrayed my dignity. The class roared with laughter and some even applauded the clever remark of the teacher. She silenced the class and continued: 'I guess we will never know the answer.' I stood up and said: 'The answer is that all the Jews in this class *are* cleverer.' The most difficult part was to begin, but once that was over I had no problem in continuing. I view myself as a person who is not easily angered, but once provoked, I become heedless of the consequences. There was such a silence in the class that my heartbeat could have been heard, but the teacher was not quick enough to intervene as I continued my expressions of outrage at her remark. She tried to stop me by trying to pacify me, saying that she did not mean anything bad by her question, but I would not be mollified. With the help of some of the older boys, she threw me out of the class.

I was reinstated after Mother went to speak to the teacher, who, of course, minimized her part by accusing me of being hypersensitive and lying about not knowing how to read and write. The fact is that I was never asked that question. My parents believed my side of the story but felt it was inadvisable to take any action. It would not serve my purpose to try to have the teacher dismissed on the charge of anti-Semitism. I asked to be transferred to a higher class but the teacher vetoed that idea, claiming that I was not ready for that. Maybe that was true, but she certainly could not teach me anything more. We managed to coexist by ignoring each other. I must admit that I learned an important lesson even from this unfortunate incident: that education is based on what you learn and not so much on what you are being taught, and by whom. I spent my days in depressing boredom, facing a person who I detested. At least I was reprieved of an extra day, because on Saturdays my parents supported my absence. This was my introduction to school and mercifully, it did not last a full term.

While trying to open a tin can, Mother accidentally cut the index finger of her right hand, with the jagged lid. She washed and bandaged it and thought nothing of it: the pain persisted, however, and it became very swollen. Eventually she went to see an army doctor, who applied some medication but was not particularly concerned by the sight of it, even though it had resulted from a cut and should have healed by now. Mother suffered from pain, the finger remained crooked and swollen, and she returned to the same doctor. This time he became alarmed and recommended that she should go to Brest Litovsk, because he thought her finger was gangrenous. He gave her a shot of penicillin but felt she needed more qualified treatment immediately. Mother insisted that she could make the trip alone, because she was afraid of leaving us again to fend for ourselves. There was plenty of military traffic and she hitchhiked to Brest Litovsk. About a week later, Mother returned, feeling much better, but her finger remained misshapen and its appearance disturbed her for the rest of her life.

History was repeating itself. Once again Brest Litovsk was the source of tidings and Mother their bearer. This time, instead of pending doom, they held the promise of salvation. Before the war, Brest Litovsk was a crossroads and had contained many transient people. It now held similar people waiting for the final defeat of Germany – which seemed very close – so that they could return to their homelands. The news that other nations, besides Russia, were fighting and winning great battles against Germany was authenticated by people with whom Mother spoke. There was even a story that Jewish brigades from Eretz Yisroel were fighting beside the British against the Nazis. The most exciting news was about her encounter with Zionist-oriented people, who told Mother that preparations were being made to transfer illegally the survivors of the holocaust to Eretz Yisroel as soon as the war was over. In the meantime, it was crucial to remove them from Russian-occupied territory and concentrate them in the west. It was necessary, therefore, for us to be registered as Polish citizens, if we intended to join in this exodus. There was no doubt as to what our intentions were, although it was beyond our imagination how our wishes were to be accomplished.

A NEW ODYSSEY IS HATCHED

Father had no problem changing the data on our registration form, stating our birthplace as the city of Breslau, Poland. Maybe the famous Rabbi Nachman inspired him to do that. Then we waited for the war to end.

In May 1945, there was ecstasy in Ratno as we found out that Germany had unconditionally surrendered. This was the signal to begin our new odyssey. We went to Kovel because it was closest and we knew that there were still a considerable number of Jews there. Everyone there had similar plans to ours, and soon a man contacted us, who worked unobtrusively to facilitate our progress. Those who already had papers identifying them as Polish citizens were organized into small groups and told to be ready to move at a minute's notice. The reason for small groups was not to arouse the suspicion of the local authorities.

Although officially the Russians permitted Poles to return to Poland, in effect they took their time about it. The Jewish leadership was aware of this and organized their own system of expediting this process, because every minute was precious and they knew that they did not have the luxury of waiting for official channels to permit the exodus. It was a credit to the ingenuity that is sometimes attributed to our people. It took about two weeks, until one evening we were told to go to the train station. About ten of us were quickly and quietly pushed into a freight car and told not to worry; we would be taken care of on the way and we must maintain silence whenever the train came to a halt. The instructions were repeated several times and the door of the freight car was closed.

As the freight train began to move, the whistle of the engine and the rumble of the wheels breaking the silence of the night, I felt a mixture of elation and fear as the train carried us into the uncertainty of the future. The mixture of elation and fear stemmed from my realization that I was leaving my country, in which I was born but which did not want me. I was heading towards fulfilling my dream of living in Eretz Yisroel. The fear was not of the hardships which lay ahead but of the possibility that we could be prevented from pursuing our goal. Was this what our survival and freedom was all about? Father, as was always his custom when setting out on a journey, recited T'filat Haderech, thanked God for saving our lives and prayed for courage to continue with what we were about to face.

At first, I heard Mother sobbing quietly in the dark, and when we asked her what was wrong, she tearfully revealed to us the sadness of her heart. Only a number of years ago we led a full life with our families and friends. It was difficult at times and extremely backwards, but we had also tasted its joys and rewards, and never realized the potential that it had to offer. She cried bitterly as she reminded us that her father had given up on America in order to lead a better Jewish life in Kortiless. We were leaving behind a shattered past and loved ones who had perished. We did not even know where some of them were buried and we would never be able to visit their graves. Now only bitter and terrible memories of Mother's birthplace would haunt her.

These freight trains were carrying spoils of war into Russia that significantly bolstered her economy. They traveled empty to the west and returned to Russia with everything that people could lay their hands on. They stripped anything that was removable and useful many of these spoils were not used, because people did not know how to use them or did not have the facilities in Russia to make them functional again. Sometimes entire factories were uprooted and transferred but never re-erected. They formed depots conveniently located near railways and delivered it home, even if not everything necessarily belonged to the German government. There was a special branch of the armed forces, which was in charge of these activities. From stories I heard later, the technical and administrative requirements of this branch were such that it included the talents of many Jews. These people were in a position to help in this secret exodus, as well non-Jews who were sympathetic to our cause. There were always those who were in a position to help if the price was right. Bribes were important because it implicated them and thus purchased their silence.

The details, which I still remember from my own experience, filled me with awe at the genius behind the operation of moving us into the west. This was a clandestine undertaking, moving the most difficult cargo of all – people. Every plan was worked out in detail and then a contingency plan was prepared, and when either failed, there was always good old chutzpah (gall).

It was daylight when the train made its first stop. We had no idea where we were and where we were heading. The door was opened and we were told in Polish, by a man wearing a railway uniform, that we could get off to stretch our legs. We were shown a place where we could wash and perform our biological functions, but warned that we should not stray from the train. We also discovered that there were more people like us on the train, so there were about fifty of us milling about quietly in the rail yard. Eventually a man appeared with another small group of refugees. This man was evidently in charge. Although previously everybody had kept silent, as soon as there was somebody in authority, the complaints came pouring out. The man behaved patiently and at times forcefully, as he answered questions and responded to complaints in Yiddish, Polish and Russian. First he weeded out the people who were unable to continue with the trip for medical and other reasons. He told us to be patient: that food would arrive and be distributed and that no one should dare to grab any of it. Evidently such behavior had to be curbed from the beginning. When he noticed my father, who had managed to organize a minyan, conducting the morning services in the yard, he quickly told him that such a thing was not possible in public, for the safety of the group, and that they should move to the confines of the freight car. Such was our freedom!

The food came and was distributed as promised. We were told to get on the train and it began to move. It was evidently not in any particular hurry to reach whatever destination it was heading for. There were stops at all kinds of hours and places, with a repetition of the same activity as at the initial stop. New human cargo was added or removed, food distributed, instructions relayed and then we were on the way again. To say that conditions were difficult is to state the obvious, but we were encouraged by hope and by the promise that soon our journey would be over. How soon that would be, however, nobody promised us.

AN OFFICER BECOMES A FLY IN THE OINTMENT

Some days later the train came to a halt in a large rail yard, in the city of Lublin. We expected the usual procedure, but this time we were warned to keep quiet and the doors remained closed. Unfortunately, a lady in one of the cars was in the process of giving birth, and her excruciating labor pains resulted in screams which did not escape the ears of a Russian officer, who was not party to the scheme. His duty was to load from the depot onto the platform and into freight cars. When he heard the screams, coming from a freight car which was marked on the outside, to show that it already contained cargo, he ordered it to be opened, as well as the rest of the cars marked in a similar way. Within a short time, all of us were standing under the watchful eyes of his soldiers, while the officer, angry and confused, tried to get to the bottom of this situation that had fallen into his hands.

We were forewarned that in the event of a confrontation such as this we were not to divulge any information beyond the fact that we were going home, and that was to be done in Polish. The help of an interpreter did not advance the officer's knowledge of how we had got into these sealed freight cars. What he was going to do with us, the officer did not know, but he proclaimed out loud, adding some juicy profanities, that Siberia would be a proper destination. To us it did not sound like an idle threat and the possibility of such a thing happening was not remote. The reason that no one, as yet, had come to bail us out was that it took time to initiate an alternative plan. We were not aware of that and became quite distressed. The first sign of hope materialized when some civilians in the company of a higher-ranking Russian officer and some soldiers approached the arresting officer. One of the civilians produced an official-looking paper stating that a consignment of human cargo was to be placed into his hands. These were Polish citizens who, as a reward for their contributions to Russia, were entitled to early repatriation. The new officer commended his comrade for his vigilance in executing his duty and told him that this incident would be fully noted before his superiors.

At the same time he suggested that the first officer should return to his duties of loading the train, and not waste any more of his valuable time on these civilians. While this exchange was going on, we were quickly broken up into small groups and told to follow one of the civilians, before the arresting officer could regain control and begin asking questions to satisfy his own curiosity. Within a short time we were spread out in various hiding places in the city, especially in the few Jewish homes.

On the same night, we were gathered together and put on

a different train to continue our journey. After what seemed like a very short trip, the train stopped. It was hot and stuffy in the car and mercifully someone opened the doors, as we were told that we would be staying here at least until the morning. In the morning, word got around that we were parked right in front of the Maydanck concentration camp. We knew nothing of the concentration camps, and my family and I joined a large group of people who had decided to visit this factory of death. I was 10 years old and I needed no explanations to understand the gruesome story, when I saw what this place contained. There were two survivors of the camp, in our group, who filled in the details. Almost a year after its liberation, it stood silent and abandoned, as if in this way the atrocities perpetrated in this place would be forgotten. The crematorium, the remnants of the electrified fence, barbed wire, barracks, hanging posts and many other signs of the destruction of human life were still there, as witnesses to the cruelty of an 'enlightened' people capable of creating a human hell.

Our trip ended several days later in the city of Katowice. There we were placed in private homes. I do not know how or by whom these homes were picked and if it was prearranged with the hosts. But the manner in which it was done and the fact that we were housed with a German family makes me believe that the hosts had little choice. We were brought to a large home and the woman who greeted us was told to give us accommodation for an indefinite period. Although the home was spacious, we lived in mutual discomfort because of our recent history. We were allotted a certain amount of money, by the people who brought us, for our food, and we had some rubles – which were legal tender even in Poland at that time – that we had saved in Ratno. How strange are the events of life. For years we were hunted and killed by these people and now we were living under the same roof 'enjoying their hospitality'. There was only the woman and two children. Somehow we coexisted and eventually the woman and Mother began to talk. It was the woman who complained of her bitter lot and the fact that her husband was a prisoner in Russia. When Mother began to relate to the woman what happened to us, she actually cried in sympathy and explained that they had never heard about any of this – only that the Jews were being transferred. When Mother explained that the transfer consisted of a torturous route to the next world, the woman was genuinely distressed.

One day, her husband returned from prison in, Russia and seeing him still wearing the German uniform was a shock for us. The man insisted that he had never participated in anything as shameful as genocide, and that he was captured early in the war and held in prison all this time. It did not matter to me whether this man participated in the atrocities. I remembered the two soldiers who were kind to us and took care of us during the Saturday round-up of the Jews of Kortiless. Yet seeing this man wearing the uniform of this cruel and dastardly Nazi 'super race' was sufficient to arouse our antipathy.

We stayed in Katowice long enough for me to begin speaking Polish quite well. The idea that we were free and yet must continue to live on handouts, provided regularly by the organization which took care of us, was abhorrent to my parents, but we had little choice. The money that we had managed to save in Ratno was already spent. The organization that took care of us obviously had financial resources. Each time it was a different person from the organization who located us and offered us money for subsistence. We had no idea who these people were or where to find them. They continually told us to have patience: they would tell us when to be ready to move at an instant's notice. It was ridiculous for Father even to try to gain employment. He tried to establish contact with the local Jewish community and went to look for a synagogue. There were the ruins of a synagogue but no trace of a Jewish community. At first my brother and I enjoyed the excitement of discovering life in a big city. Occasionally we even traveled alone on long streetcar rides. That excitement, however, began to wear off, as I felt that this was not what I had hoped for and I was not interested in the city becoming part of my future. When we were on the verge of losing hope that we would ever leave this place, the good news finally came – not that I was looking forward to the terrible freight car rides again, but I was anxious to begin a new life and to feel that I had arrived at my destination. That was sufficient reason to be excited about continuing our trip.

ONE DAY I WAKE UP TO DISCOVER THAT I AM GREEK

We received new identification papers, and this time not only was our birthplace incorrect, but also our names sounded Greek to me. Actually, I did not know what Greek names were supposed to sound like, but these names really were Greek and we had to memorize them and respond only to them. We eventually found out what was behind this charade. Now that everyone was free, the French were returning to France, the Poles to Poland, the Greeks to Greece, but the Jews had no place to go. The British White Paper made sure of that. We could not declare that we were heading for Eretz Yisroel (Palestine). Why? Neither the east nor the 'friendly west' was interested, for political reasons, in the Jews going to Palestine. Whoever was left of the recently-liberated Jews of Poland, Ukraine and the rest of eastern Europe did manage to travel, but not as Jews. Jews had no business to travel because they had no destination that was officially recognized by the rest of the world community.

Since the rules of the game were stacked against the Jewish survivors, our leadership decided to create their own means whereby these rules could be circumvented. The objective was to bring as many as possible of the survivor as close as possible to the shores of Israel. This meant reaching ports on the shores of the Mediterranean and from there boarding an illegal ship to Eretz Yisroel. Since Greeks who had been interned in concentration camps in eastern Europe would have to take the same route in order to return to their homeland, we were now their impostors. This was Jewish ingenuity or chutzpah, and for the most part it worked.

GO WEST, YOUNG MAN

As 'genuine' Greeks, we boarded a passenger train headingd for the city of Prague. But we did not know any Greek. No problem: Hebrew would serve just as well. But who knew Hebrew? No problem: just quote anything you remember by heart from the prayer book. But what if you did not know any prayers? Then, just shut up. Accompanying us was a man who spoke the local language, plus Russian, and was equipped to handle any contingency. Somewhere along the line, a Russian officer, obviously drunk, boarded the train and chose our section of the car. My father caught his attention, maybe because he was standing at the side and silently reciting his morning prayers, although without a tallith and tefillin, because he could not yet obtain any. It is doubtful, however, that the officer suspected my father of praying, because in the drunken state he was in, he could not have told the difference between prayer and parody. After a while he decided that my father was not Greek (which was true) but a Gruzinian defector from the Russian army (absolutely false). Father, of course, understood what the officer was saying and responded with a wide range of quotations from the scriptures, which could have had him ordained as a rabbi but did not convince the officer of his Greek lineage. When the train made a stop and the officer descended, we assumed that this was the end, but the officer returned with a genuine Greek to face my father. The dialogue between the two of them was not getting anywhere – maybe my father's dialect was strange to the Greek – and at that point, the man who was in charge of us intervened. He managed to convince the officer that my father had classical Greek swarthy features, which made it impossible for him to be Gruzinian, and that the man he had brought could not be a real Greek because he was blond. The officer was sufficiently confused by the doubletalk of our leader and his ability to converse with everyone in their own languages, including Greek, and to exchange scriptural quotations with my father, that he decided to abandon the train, with the Greek in tow. We were sure that eventually the Greek would succeed in convincing the officer of his authenticity as a Greek much better than my father had. Fortunately the train started to move and we breathed in relief that this brief, comical but potentially dangerous episode was over. That took chutzpah.

In Prague, our group was added to an already-existing group, housed in a large building which may have been a hotel at one time. Simply-prepared food and at least one warm meal a day was supplied to us. The general atmosphere was more relaxed and there was even a movie house near by, showing Russian propaganda features. Previously the people who had made our trip possible remained anonymous and constantly rotated, but now the same people remained ever present and even had names. They began the task of organizing us into small cells of ten to fifteen people, and conducted orientation sessions. The purpose of these sessions was for us to become acquainted with each other, because we were going to continue our journey together. It was a means of informing us bluntly of the difficulties which still lay ahead. Most important of all, for the first time we began to receive news from Eretz Yisroel, from a man who, we were told, came from there. Nothing could have crystallized or given more substance to our dream than meeting this man and although it was premature to become euphoric, it was enough of a reason to be happy.

To add to our happiness, there was a chance meeting between my mother and a second cousin from a small town in the Ukraine, who was the only survivor (apart from us) of our substantial family in that country. She was a beautiful girl in her late teens, and her story of survival was another episode which could be attributed to a combination of the strength of the human spirit and the strange workings of fate. Our reunion did not last long because we were informed that our group was to set out again, but we promised to meet in Eretz Yisroel. Happily, I was the first one of my family to keep that promise.

The coming leg of the journey took us – still in possession of our Greek identities – to the city of Bratislava. It is interesting to note that although we were still in the same country, the attitude of the local people was hostile, compared to the friendly and sympathetic way we were received in Prague. We were now close to the Austrian border and the city of Vienna, which was our real objective, but for some reason we could not continue. Because new people were constantly arriving, our accommodation was becoming cramped, food supplies meager and tempers short. Eventually we found ourselves travelling with our group, not to Vienna but to Budapest. It was a long, exhausting journey and to add to my family's troubles, I became very sick. I was 10 years old but looked more like 6 or 7. The main symptom of my malady was a very high fever and I complained of needles pricking my skin, and I hallucinated. In this state, I could not preserve my Greek identity and revealed my capacity for languages as I carried on with my visions, in Russian, Yiddish, Ukrainian and my recently- acquired Polish. Some medical attention was obtained and I was given something to reduce my fever. I stretched out on the baggage rack and was made secure – there was no other available space – and in these conditions, with the constant care and worry of my family, the trip continued.

When we reached Budapest, I was almost blind. That is, I could distinguish shades of light and even discern hazily my parents' faces, but it was painful to keep my eyes open. I was taken to the hospital, which was close to the place where my parents and the rest of the group stayed. What brought on my condition I never found out, but with care, after about a month, my sight was completely restored. There was a Jewish–Hungarian man next to me in the hospital. The only language he spoke was Hungarian. Even in my state, I became aware that this language was nothing like any I had ever heard before. It had its own rhythm, contrary to the Slavic beat, and even when he said my name, the accent was on the wrong syllable. Before the war this man was a famous actor and pantomime artiste and although he had lost his family, he managed to survive owing to his art. To comfort and to amuse me he began, for the first time since the war, to perform pantomime sketches, and sometimes in a kind of gibberish – maybe it was Hungarian – he would play all kinds of characters. A wonderful friendship developed which turned out to be beneficial to both of us and in which the spoken word, between friends, was not essential. It was the first time that I became aware of theatre art and a love for it remained with me.

The group with which we had traveled since Prague could not wait for my complete recuperation and went on its way. Father managed to acquire a *taless* and a pair of *tefillin*, acquisitions that only my complete recovery could rival in his happiness. From this point on, Father declared that he would no longer eat food unless he was certain that it was kosher, particularly meat.

Finally we crossed into Austria and reached the city of Vienna. I knew that we were in the west because this was the first time I saw an American soldier, and he was black. Once again we were set up in relatively spacious accommodation, which must have been a hotel, and a ceremony took place, in which a speaker congratulated us on our achievement of reaching the west. I failed to see what our part was in the achievement because we were like sheep following expert and capable shepherds. Our Greek ID papers were collected, probably to be used with a new batch of refugees. Cards were issued instead, in our real names, that also entitled us to food rations. We were told that after we had rested for a while, we would be reassigned to various places in Austria, where we would stay until we could be taken to our final destination: Eretz Yisroel.

5 Home is a DP Camp

In the late fall of 1945, we reached a place called Bindermichel, near the city of Linz. This was a community built by the Germans for army personnel and their families. It was constructed with military precision, in long train-like blocks. Each block contained anything from four to ten entrances, and each entrance contained four homes. We lived in Block 14, Entrance 10 and Home 1 until June 1948.

By the time we arrived, there were well over fifteen hundred people and at peak times more than two thousand. Upon arrival, registration took place. The interesting part about registration in a Displaced Persons (DP) Camp is that essentially everyone could, and in many cases did, assume vital details that were to their liking. No details had to be substantiated because the papers with which they traveled were themselves a fabrication. My own date of birth was created with the help of the clerk making the registration. My mother hesitated for a moment, trying to convert from the Hebrew calendar to the Gregorian. She started hesitantly: 'It was around Passover ...', and the man completed by saying, 'He looks about 8 years old.' At this point Mother lost her patience with the intervening clerk and told the man to write down 18 March 1935. As for place of birth, no one had ever heard of a quaint place like Kortiless. Consequently Ratno was chosen, being the closest identifiable city to the village. ID and food ration cards were given out. The ration cards had to be renewed each month. I finally found out who my keepers were and what my status was. My 'father' was UNRWA

(United Nations Relief and Welfare Agency) and my 'mother' was JOINT (American Joint Distribution Committee) and my status was DP. That was quite an accomplishment for a little Jewish boy from Kortiless. UNRWA fed me and JOINT took care of all my other needs, and I should have been a happy little boy, enjoying, during my formative years, the luxury of such good care and attention. However, the stigma of being a DP pretty much spoiled everything. I had no complaints against UNRWA or JOINT because they certainly tried to do the best for us. One of the most admirable accomplishments of JOINT was to locate our relatives and acquaintances in the Western Hemisphere. This was done after my parents filled out a form given to us, indicating the names and places where these people were supposed to be. Within about a year we began to receive letters from them. One disappointment was that we had not, as yet, reached our objective, and although we were going through the motions of setting up all the institutions which normal life demanded, they were all on a temporary basis. Besides, who was to decide what normal life was? Under the circumstances our existence was relatively normal.

BACK TO SCHOOL ONCE AGAIN

The first institution that any community needed was a school. For the second time in my short life I was being tested for my qualifications in the academic world. This time I volunteered information and told them that I went to cheder until the age of 6 and that I knew how to read Hebrew and also knew how to read and write Russian. In my enthusiasm to prove how clever I was, I recited the prayer of 'Adon Olam' (Master of the universe) by heart and even sang a Yiddish song. It seemed to impress some of the students and teachers present at this audition. When I was asked if I knew anything else and I told them, 'Nothing', they smiled, shook their heads sadly and said that I would be informed as to which class I had been assigned. For some reason, the question about whether I knew anything else rubbed me up the wrong way. It was as if they were intimating that everything I did know was useless. There were, in fact, no such things as classes based on your knowledge, because very few of us had had the opportunity of attending school, so the main criterion for which group you belonged to was your age range. Since there was another group below me, I assumed I was in grade two.

The official language of instruction was Yiddish. Although all the people in the camp came from eastern Europe, not everyone spoke the language, in particular the children. A number of us were in the fortunate position of knowing how to speak Yiddish, but not how to read and write it, although I did know how to read. That alone gave me the feeling that I knew everything, which invariably landed me in trouble with the teacher. The teacher came from Galicia, and to my ear his pronunciation of certain words was offensive. I used to relieve the boredom of studying the basics of the Yiddish language, by starting arguments – in which I am now sure that the teacher was right – and they eventually caused me to become persona non grata in his course. I had to learn writing Yiddish, on my own. The first book that I read in Yiddish was a translation of Kipling's *The Jungle Book*.

MY SHORT MUSICAL CAREER

The curriculum was not set up by a pedagogical committee and was not sternly adhered to. It usually depended on how long the teacher of a certain subject remained in camp. In many cases, when the teacher left the camp and there was no one to replace him, the subject became defunct. In the case of Hebrew, geography of Eretz Yisroel and Jewish history, all efforts were invested to keep the courses running. New subjects were constantly introduced and old ones deleted by the Zipper principal. That was the name of the principal of the school. I was not a good student, for two reasons: poor study habits – because I never had a chance to acquire proper ones – and a constant discipline problem. I can claim in all modesty, however, that I excelled in the subjects I liked, which happened to be the above-mentioned ones. This did not prevent me, however, from becoming embroiled in unfortunate discipline incidents with some of the teachers. Our music teacher, who was a short, round little woman who spoke only Polish, insisted upon teaching me to read music because she thought I had a beautiful voice. I did not mind the singing but decided that it was a waste of my time to learn the names and sounds of the various markings. To me they looked like tracks left by chickens with dirty feet. She was not pleased when I expressed this opinion of sheet music. She was even less pleased when she was trying to teach the class while I was trying to make it giddy. This was not too difficult a task, and when she caught me in the act of my misdemeanor, she decided to have it out with me. In her high soprano voice (I never liked sopranos) she told me, in cultured Polish, what she thought of me. Maybe in Polish it took longer to say. The class happened to be standing around the piano and I was near the rod that supported the lid. The teacher, in order to be seen, stood up and placed both hands on the rim of the piano to gain some additional height. I cannot deny that it was I who moved the rod, which made the lid fall, that cut her harangue short with an ear-splitting screech, and made her sit down to catch her breath – which made her even shorter – and all of which shortened my music career. At the time, of course, I denied being responsible for this mishap, but since rods supporting piano lids are not in the habit of falling of their own accord, it was only natural to assume that I was the force behind it. In short, unfortunately, I never learned to read music.

NOTHING MATTERS AS LONG AS YOU ARE HEALTHY

There were many excuses and reasons for my underachievement, particularly in subjects which I disliked and found difficult or vice versa. The state of my health was a good reason. The condition of many of the DPs, particularly the children, was such that they required constant medical attention. Not to miss out on a good thing, I aptly qualified for this care. I was small, emaciated and regularly afflicted with some kind of malady: stomach aches, swollen glands, toothaches, colds; and if there was some kind of children's disease around, I was among the first to bear its signs. My condition entitled me to special food rations that included cans of Carnation condensed milk. Consuming the gooey, sweet stuff was the good part but the bad part was that my illnesses contributed to the chip on my shoulder. In general I had a happy disposition, with a tendency for mischief and fun that earned me the nickname of *Payatz* (clown), amongst my friends – a name that I gladly accepted because I had earned it and tried to live up to it. To add to my woes, I began to suffer from terrible nightmares. They were like reruns of my war experiences. I saw myself standing before a German firing squad; lost in the woods, in search of my parents or facing a menacing wolf; or falling from some high place into an abyss; and other frightening situations that would cause me to scream in my sleep. The result was that not only was my sleep interrupted but also that of my parents, who spent hours trying to comfort me and assure me that I was facing no danger.

The doctors decided that my condition emanated from malnutrition and other punishments to which my body had been subjected during the war. I was a perfect candidate for a resort camp that had been established somewhere in the mountains of upper Austria, for children, from all the DP camps located in that country, who were similar wrecks like myself. We were the *Nebbechs* (unfortunates) of the DPs and we were entitled to the best. There were a good number of us, of assorted ages, gathered at a large, beautiful villa near a lake called Wolfgang. We were under the constant supervision of doctors and nurses and practically force-fed, like geese.

INDOCTRINATION AND RECUPERATION

Our education was not neglected. Once again I was being classified, and found myself studying subjects such as algebra, while simple mathematics was still a mystery to me, and English, without knowing the Latin alphabet. There were a number of older boys and girls, in their late teens, who were sent from Israel and served as counselors for various activities. The counselor in charge of the group of boys to which I belonged was a politically-astute revisionist, belonging to the Beitar Party (that is what I call him today: then I thought he was just a bully). He spent all his time with us, subjecting us to indoctrination, military discipline and martial arts with sticks. The only enjoyable part, for me, was that he taught us nationalistic Beitar songs. At first I did not like this activity: maybe I did not like having my knuckles bruised or the strict atmosphere which it imposed upon me, and consequently I avoided participating. Social pressure, however, changed my mind, and I gradually became an enthusiastic participant, at the same time absorbing a revisionist political orientation. Jabotinsky became my hero and both sides of the Jordan River my goal.

I returned home two months later, physically in much better shape than when I left. My classmates received me royally but I discovered that there was a wide gap between what they were sudying and what I had managed to learn. When I boasted to the math teacher (my nemesis) that I knew algebra – something that my class had not as yet gone into – he called upon me to solve a problem. I stood helplessly, without the faintest idea of how to apply the equations that I had learned by heart. Sternly, he informed me that I had a lot of catching up to do and added the admonition that a little knowledge was a dangerous thing. It was not a comfortable position to be in but I managed to redeem myself in the eyes of the class, during recess, by presenting them with a hilarious demonstration of my knowledge of the English language. My English vocabulary was very limited but my comments and description of how one has to pretend to be holding a hot potato in the mouth while speaking the language produced the desired results.

A DP CAMP IS A DYNAMIC ENTITY

Things changed rapidly in a transient camp. In the two months that I had been away, new teachers and classmates had arrived and old ones had left. Those who had left included my former music teacher, whom I did not mind losing, but also two boys and a girl of whom I was particularly fond. That bothered me for a while but I consoled myself with the fact that since they had gone to America, they were no longer important to me. At this stage, only single and young people were encouraged to move on, to reach the illegal ships which would take them to Eretz Isroel. Most of us declared ourselves Zionists and waited for the opportunity to go to Israel; those who left for other destinations became instant traitors. My newfound nationalistic political orientation made my attitude towards such people even more negative.

My political zeal and expounding of revisionist theories, of which I had limited knowledge and understanding, were sources of amusement for my parents and my brother. Carefully, and with all the artistic talent that I could muster, I drew the logo of the Beitar Party on the wall near my bed and hung a large picture of Jabotinsky next to it. No doubt I made myself obnoxious, at least to those who were opposed to the Beitar view, with my advocation of an Eretz Isroel that would encompass both sides of the Jordan. To drive the point home, I would burst into a song bearing that message.

My revisionist zeal came to an abrupt end one day, when we found our camp surrounded by American soldiers, conducting a house-to-house search for Beitar activists. Betarniks trying to steal arms had penetrated an American army camp. A guard discovered them and in the confrontation the guard was badly hurt and some weapons were stolen. The action was reprehensible and had adverse repercussions. All refugee movements were severely limited, especially those heading towards Mediterranean ports to reach illegal ships. Besides causing a rift with the American authorities, this incident became a source of tension amongst Jews as well. In spite of the fact that the operation was blamed on some hotheads, it was certainly the Beitar Party that was behind it. My enthusiasm for the Beitar Party disappeared much more quickly than it had grown. By the time the American soldiers brusquely invaded my house, in search of the weapons and suspected participants in the raid, all signs of my Beitar affiliation had disappeared from the wall and from my life.

TWO JEWS CAN FORM THREE POLITICAL PARTIES

Had I continued to live in Kortiless, I would have labored under the assumption that all Jews are alike, in the sense that they possess the exceptional quality of being their brother's keeper. I would have continued to believe that a common goal and concern for the welfare and perpetuation of the Jewish people united them. I was now thousands of miles away from Kortiless, and after being exposed to a great variety of Jews, I became convinced that I was equally as far off course from my initial assumption. I now believed that Jews were heterogeneous. The disparaging joke about bringing together two Jews and forming at least three political parties was a fact of life in the DP camps. There were parties from left to right on the political scale and even religious parties, each with their own political hues and, of course, their own synagogue. In addition, there were also apolitical *Landsmanschaften*, organizations based on their places or countries of origin. The self-styled community and party leaders used every opportunity, particularly public functions, to make long, blustering speeches to gain prominence for themselves and the party they represented. Any attempt at limiting the number of speeches or curtailing in any way the exposure of some group resulted in bitter arguments and charges of discrimination. The democratic process of elections was introduced and that resulted in even greater rifts and animosities. I discovered that Jews were capable of slandering each other, cheating, pressuring and, most appalling of all, even using force. The chosen people were no different to any other nation, except that at the time, we were a nation without a country.

Probably the most horrendous experience to witness during this period was when fate brought into confrontation two Jews who had survived the horrors of a concentration camp. Although both of them had been inmates, one of them had been there in the capacity of *kapo* (inmate policeman). In most cases, although powerless themselves, these 'policemen' tried to help in whatever way they could, but there were also those who betrayed, abused and added to the suffering of their fellow Jews. This particular incident happened at a public function. While someone was addressing the audience, a sudden disturbance broke out in a section of the hall. There was hysterical shouting and the man who was doing the shouting was knocked down to the floor. He quickly got up and ran to the podium and yelled, '*Kapo!*' He pointed at a man who stood, white faced, at the back of the hall, and began to relate a tale of horrors in which this *kapo* was involved. The people were ready to lynch the *kapo* but it was his accuser who intervened. He only wanted people to know what kind of animal this man was and, if he had a conscience, that he should continue to live and suffer the consequences of his degradation. Evidently the man did have a conscience after all, because some time later he committed suicide.

POLITICAL AFFILIATION

My father was a Chassid in his lifestyle, attitude and religious observance, but he never identified himself with the court of any particular rabbi. When asked with whom he was affiliated, he would answer, cryptically, 'To the Maker of the universe.' In all fairness, there were many who avoided being identified with any political organization, and the only thing which interested them was the blessed day on which they could leave the camp and be on their way to Eretz Yisroel. This was a goal which, essentially, united most of us, and everyone seemed to be laboring for that common purpose. There were those, however, who claimed that they offered the right way to achieve that goal. There were also many who were interested in reaching *di goldene medineh* (the golden state), America. The polarization within the ranks of the Jews bothered me: I became aware of it after my short stint of identifying with the Beitar movement. Although I became conscious of various political orientations, for a long time I steered away from any political activity. Except for Zionist activities without any shades of political overtones, the school was off-limits for political or religious involvement. For those of us who were religious, there was a cheder and, of course, I attended it.

REB (MR) MOSES THE ENLIGHTENED

The name of my rebbe was Reb Moses, who was pompous, trimmed his beard, wore a very little yarmulke and was a strict, no-nonsense disciplinarian. There were a number of differences between him and my rebbe in Kortiless. Reb Moses never pulled or twisted our ears when he felt that a point had to be driven home or our behavior had to be corrected. He had an enlightened technique of patting our cheeks and finishing the action with a vise-like pinch, which would send needle-sharp pain through the body and tears to the eyes. My rebbe in Kortiless may have twisted our ears but at the same time he had a fondness for every one of us and a sincere interest in our studies. The 'love pat' of Reb Moses looked harmless on the surface, but for us it more than bordered on molestation. Another weapon in his arsenal of pedagogical practices was cursing us when angered. Aside from these idiosyncrasies, he was not a very pleasant man but he was a good teacher and I was anxious to learn. According to him, our being behind in the study of the Torah because of the war was no excuse and we had to apply ourselves to catch up as quickly as possible to the level which our age dictated. It was he who decided what our level should be and kept driving us towards it. Without permitting time for discussion or for questions that may have had overtones of dissension, we studied Rashi, Gmarah and the weekly portions of the Pentateuch. The only time he would deviate from this course was when he launched into long tirades about wasting our time in pursuit of activities like sports, performances, public functions and even attending school. In brief, as far as he was concerned, it was only what *he* had to teach us that was essential: the rest was irrelevant.

HAKOACH BINDERMICHEL VERSUS LASK
(LINZER ATLETISCHER SPORTS KLUB)

Amongst the survivors there were some excellent athletes in various fields of sports, and owing to their endeavors, money was allocated to establish the Hakoach Sports Klub. For me, the world of sports was a wonderful discovery. There was soccer, ping-pong, volleyball, swimming, gymnastics and even chess. The popularity of each branch depended largely on the presence of a star athlete in a certain field because when he or she departed, the interest would fade. Soccer (football) remained consistently popular and there was even an adult team, which participated in Austrian lower league games. I was an ardent fan and tried to attend every game, even those that took place far from Linz. Unfortunately, some of the games were held on Shabbat. It was bad enough to watch a soccer game on Shabbat, which I brought myself to do with a guilty conscience. To travel in a vehicle on Shabbat was out of the question. Despite my overwhelming desire to see the game, I would stand at the side, watching my friends as they boarded the bus or truck which would take them to the game, sorely tempted to join them.

One Saturday afternoon, as I was observing the last passengers boarding the bus, I was dumbstruck to see Reb Moses' son appear. He glanced furtively to the sides, removed his yarmulke and boarded the bus. Although I did not remove my cap, I boarded the bus right behind him.

Rebbe Moses would always make a point, in his tirades against wasting time in useless pursuits, of upholding his son (who was a number of years older than us) as a shining example of piety and accomplishment. None of us liked his son because we knew him as a pretentious bully and hypocrite, but none of us dared to contradict the rebbe. I now stood behind this shining example, my heart full of regret for my sin of riding on Shabbat to see a soccer game. He was not the least uncomfortable at this confrontation but looked at me as if I was the only perpetrator of the sin. I miserably avoided his stare and hardly enjoyed the game because of remorse for what I had done. At least I was certain that he could not snitch on me to the rebbe without implicating himself. I was wrong.

Father returned from Saturday evening prayers and confronted me with the fact, which he had learned from my rebbe, that I had profaned the Shabbat. The pained look of disappointment in me and the anger in his face, coupled with the fact that I had lied to him about my whereabouts, were sufficient reasons for my feeling miserable and at the same time, I was relieved that I had been found out and had to face my punishment. Tearfully I admitted my transgressions and promised, with all sincerity, that I would not travel again on Shabbat – a promise I kept until the age of 18.

I anticipated and prepared myself for the moralizing and tongue-lashing of the rebbe. The worst part was over because I had settled my differences with Father – in fact, I was very angry at the rebbe for having confronted my father first instead of me. The rebbe declared that before beginning the lesson, he had an unpleasant duty to perform. After carrying on for a while about the terrible consequences of sin, and saying that such a sinner was present in the room, he pointed a finger at me and began to curse and upbraid me for my unforgivable behavior. I was comforted by the fact that I had been forgiven by my father. It was unpleasant to be degraded in such a manner, but since I was guilty, I sat silently, although my anger steadily increased. I knew, of course, how the rebbe had obtained the information but I asked him anyway. His reply was that he had his reliable sources and it did not matter, who told him. 'To me it matters' I cried out, choking on my tears. I was angry at the evil betrayal, which had caused unnecessary pain to my father and humiliated me. I continued, unmindful of the consequences: 'It was your son! He was with me on the bus!' Then I divulged the rest of the details. The rebbe stood speechless for a minute, turned red in the face and was about to strike me. I yelled out, 'It is true!', and he stopped and told us to go home.

Undoubtedly the confrontation between the rebbe and his son must have been traumatic, because the latter threatened that if he ever caught me alone, he would teach me a lesson I would never forget. He probably would have done so, if I had not warned him that if he ever laid a hand on me, I would expose him at services in the synagogue, revealing that he had traveled on Shabbat to a soccer game. I returned to my studies in cheder the following day. I continued to play soccer but never traveled on Shabbat, and the rebbe stopped using his son as an example of piety.

Aside from the athletes amongst us, there were also artists in various fields. Having been exposed to theatre by my actor and mime friend in the Budapest hospital, I remained partial to it. Surviving members of the Rumanian and Polish Yiddish theatres formed a theatre group. Because of their meager means, they never presented full-length plays but concentrated on satirical sketches dealing with camp life and world events, comical impressions of local personalities, and song and dance numbers. These shows were enthusiastically received by almost everyone and offered a wealth of funny material to be emulated and rehashed by budding artists like myself. My rebbe was sternly opposed to the theatre and warned us against attending, on the pain of expulsion or the alternative, receiving his 'love pats'. At first I did not attend – that is, I did not go inside the large barrack in which the show took place – but I found a convenient crack or window from where I could watch. After the 'Shabbat incident', however, I no longer allowed the Rebbe to influence my behavior outside the cheder, as long as I obtained my parents' permission. Well, to be completely honest, occasionally even without their permission.

AS IT STANDS WRITTEN ...

Another result of 'the incident' was that it diminished my fear of the rebbe. Whereas before, I was docile and endured his pinching and cursing, now I was on the alert for the oncoming pinch and escaped his reach, which would make his cursing even more ferocious. Having overcome my docility made the lessons more interesting for me. The method of study was simple. The rebbe would read part of a sentence and translate it into Yiddish; we would repeat it after him and he would continue, in the style in which the Four Questions are asked at the Seder. On one occasion, while we were studying the weekly portion of the Torah, we came across the story of Lot and his daughters. The text states that each daughter, on different occasions, got her father drunk and 'lay' with him (*vatishkav eemo*). The rebbe chose to translate the passage as though Lot married his daughters. When our turn came to repeat, I said, 'slept'. Evidently he was sensitive to this passage and felt that 'married' was more fitting for this patriarch and for our ears. When he heard me, he immediately corrected me. I was confident of my translation and would not budge. By the look on his face, I anticipated a hefty pinch, but this time I was caught off guard, because I became too involved in the argument and tried to convince him with my knowledge of Hebrew. He stood next to me and said, '*Sheigetz*, when I say married, I mean married', and slapped me swiftly across the face. It was a shock, it hurt and I was insulted. I sat for a few minutes, trying to overcome my tears, and then I got up and started to walk out. The rebbe asked me where I was going and I replied, 'To look for a rebbe!' My Hebrew teacher, Mr Lev, became my new rebbe.

I DID NOT KNOW THAT 'ALL THE WORLD IS A STAGE ...'

Our neighbor, who was a very funny and cynical man, was connected to the theatre by writing much of the material. He was the only person who, for some reason, found my complications at school and cheder amusing. He would put an arm around me and say with a grin: 'Reb Laizer, if you permit silly things like that to destroy your spirit, you will never have the strength to face the difficult problems in life.' I liked the man and he thought I had talent, besides the one for getting into trouble. One day he took me to observe a rehearsal of the troupe and I was carried away with delight at watching the silly manner in which the actors were behaving. He asked me if I would mind singing a song, 'By Dem Rebben's Tish', that he had taught me. Eagerly I complied, and without even realizing that I was auditioning, I was accepted into to the troupe. All hell broke loose. The rebbe and the school, for the first time, agreed on something. They opposed my becoming a member of the troupe. Furthermore, my parents joined forces with the 'nays' and the 'nays' had it. My chance of going on stage was barred and the world was denied the benefit of my thespian talent, at least for quite a while.

A LANGUAGE IS FOR COMMUNICATION AND NOT ONLY TO BE STUDIED

In the summer of 1946 I went to a camp for the first time in my life. It was an experience which helped me to absorb new ideas and to understand of the meaning of freedom. All the children from Bindermichel were brought to a magnificent house in the mountains, surrounded by trees and located about fifty meters from a lake called Ebensee. It was a setting that defied description in its beauty, but I discovered that beauty can only really be appreciated when one is mentally and emotionally prepared to become aware of it. Although some of our teachers accompanied us, the program was conducted by three young Israelis, two men and a woman, who were sent specifically for this purpose and had the qualifications to run this kind of project. The Hebrew that they spoke amongst themselves sounded different to what we had learned at school or in cheder. It was the first time I heard people using the language to communicate amongst themselves, rather than with God. The Sephardic dialect gave a different sound to familiar words, which we pronounced in Ashkenazi tempo and emphasis. What amazed me even more was that they used the same dialect in their prayers. I immediately became a convert to Sephardic dialect and a complete devotee of the study of the Hebrew language. Even if my vocabulary was limited, I decided that I would speak Hebrew, and made an agreement with my closest friend that between ourselves, this was the language that we would use. It was a frustrating effort but we had three living dictionaries, who willingly helped us when they learned of our agreement. The Israeli counselors filled our days with a choice of endless activities: each one was a new discovery and adventure. There was Israeli folk dancing, besides the hora, which offered the body a form of expression and gave free range to the spirit that it possessed. There were songs, which I eagerly copied, learning the meaning of each word and memorizing them. These were additional credentials to my identity with my people. They were songs describing the process of building the country; heroic deeds of defending it; the beauty of certain parts of it; children's songs and those based on passages from the scriptures. For those who were interested, there was a mixed Bible study circle. The idea that girls could participate was novel in itself, but that it was conducted by a woman was to me a rare phenomenon. Until this point, the only woman I knew who was familiar with the scriptures was my mother. Once again, the heroes of the Bible assumed new stature, as our counselor not only read the contents to us but described details of the period and acted out the roles of the characters. There was always enough time for discussion and for questions. Hikes and scout craft were considered sufficiently important for Jewish boys and girls to engage in.

I was never like a sponge in my quest for knowledge, but this period was the closest that I ever came to it. The reason was not so much my thirst for knowledge but, I presume, psychological. Until now, I had met Jews who came from all the countries of Europe, even some American–Jewish soldiers, and they all had about them the aura of their country of origin. The Israelis also had an aura about them and for me, at them that time, it represented the epitome of being Jewish. I envied their birthplace. For me, there was a marked difference between a Ukrainian Jew, like myself, and a Jew who was born in Eretz Yisroel, the country of our origin. It was my desire to be like them, to emulate them in every possible way. That was the driving force behind my enthusiasm. It was they who offered me the key to my identity, and the clarity of purpose in my life made me happy.

I was stimulated by this discovery to greater awareness of myself and everything around me. For the first time, I devoted attention to the beauty surrounding our campsite. One special experience came after a hectic day of activity, which made everything right with the world. We were told to go up to our rooms to wash and then come to supper. As I came down, I happened to look in the direction of the lake, and instead of continuing to the dining room, I changed course and went down to it. The lake was smooth as glass and reflected, like a mirror, the entire vicinity. The setting sun above the crest of the mountains added another point of reference to strengthen the fact that I was observing two identical worlds. For the first time since the war, there was something more important than filling my belly. I sat down, watched the setting sun and listened admiringly to the yodeling of the Austrians. It was in this state of well-being that another thought permeated my mind: the euphoric feeling that I was a free person.

THE ROUTINE OF LIFE IN A DP CAMP

Living in camp, being provided with a ration card and the basic necessities, had an adverse effect on most adults, my father amongst them. Being by nature an energetic man, the lack of employment and the very idea of being idle bothered him. Eventually, he obtained the post of *baal tfilah* (cantor) in the synagogue that he attended. Without cantorial pretensions, but with a beautiful voice and a style of delivery which originated in the soul, he became quite popular and attendance at the synagogue increased. I do not think that there was any remuneration involved but Father was happier. JOINT set up an ORT school where Mother took some sewing courses and my brother studied to become an electrician, after he had graduated from the highest class available in the local school. We began to receive letters from our relatives in Canada and the US, offering their assistance and also suggesting that they put in requests to bring us to North America. My parents, my brother and I were opposed to the idea, of course, and thanked them for their offer but informed them that our intention was to reach Eretz Yisroel.

Families that were determined to reach Eretz Yisroel or did not have anybody in America to issue requisition papers, or were not in a class of desirables due to their profession, remained longest in the camp. The ordeal of having to say farewell to close friends kept repeating itself and emotionally it drained me to the limits. I was aware that a DP camp was a temporary world: nevertheless, close friendships are not formed on the basis of preconditions for their longevity; they are from the heart and based on the elusive word, 'forever'. For me, 'forever' came to too many abrupt and painful endings.

REDEMPTION IS ON THE WAY BUT IT'S CANADA
INSTEAD OF CANAAN

In November 1947, when the UN agreed on partition, we were ecstatic and assumed that any day we would be called upon to move. We sent most of our belongings, that we had managed to accumulate in the past years, to our relatives in Eretz Yisroel, so that it would be easier for us to travel. The British, however, seemed to have increased their vigilance, and although the Zionist leadership tried to gain world attention by its effort to run the blockade with the ship *Exodus 47*, we were left sitting in the camp. From this point on, it became the hardest period to endure, because we seemed so close to our objective, but unfortunately we were beset with the feeling of being forgotten.

May 1948 came and Eretz Yisroel became Israel. All my trials should have been over. Not true. Although free immigration to Israel was now possible priority was given to able-bodied men and women. The families would still have to linger for 'a while'. In later years I discovered that this was a direct policy from Ben-Gurion himself. At the end of the same month, my parents revealed to us that requisition papers had arrived from Canada, making us eligible for immediate departure. It was this last period that had broken their spirit, and without consulting us, they agreed on the alternative course of going to Canada. Mother's cousin in Montreal, who was a day or so older than she and bore the name of Ruttenberg – the same as my mother's maiden name – acquired papers claiming her as his twin sister. Reunion of immediate family had first priority and that meant that we were practically on the way to Canada instead of Canaan.

After all these years of waiting, and bearing the name of DP because we intended to go to Eretz Yisroel, now that it had become Israel, and after my superior airs with my friends who went to America, now I was following in the footsteps of those friends, the 'betrayers'. It was a very hard blow. I refused to accept the honor of addressing, in the name of the children in the camp, a rally for the new State of Israel, because I felt I did not deserve it. This was a task that on previous occasions I had carried out with great aplomb. I offered excuses and reasons but I knew exactly how my remaining friends felt. I had been in their position myself and I knew what it felt like. My brother offered greater resistance to the idea of going to Canada. Without my parents' knowledge, he enlisted into the Gachal (foreign volunteers brigade), by claiming that he was 18 years old, and no one bothered to verify his real age. This was a group of volunteers who received priority to be moved because they were going to fight in the War of Independence. He intended simply to run away. Somehow my parents got wind of this plan and obtained his release by revealing his real age as 16.

DESTINATION WEST INSTEAD OF EAST

In June 1948 we left Austria. The fact that most of my original friends, who knew of my devotion and love for Israel, were not around to see me follow our new route made matters much easier. Instead of feeling elated that finally I was bound for a destination that would offer me a permanent place in its society – rather than the temporary life that this abhorrent camp represented – I felt that my goal had been compromised. In spite of it all, I became resigned to my circumstance, knowing it was not much easier for my parents and especially difficult for my brother.

We were no longer under the auspices of the Zionist movement but solely the wards of JOINT and still DPs, as the tags on our person indicated. After being tagged, catalogued and identified we were placed aboard a train that took us to another camp, near the city of Torino. It must have been a former army camp because we were housed in barracks. About fifty people were housed in each barrack. There were also a central kitchen and dining room that supplied meals. Father demanded and managed to obtain some basic items of kosher food that we prepared ourselves. Although the majority was Jewish, there were people from all the nationalities of Europe, and I was receiving my first taste of the ingredients which were to become part of the melting pot.

Once again, we were subjected to waiting. The conditions here were much worse than those we had endured in Austria. There, even if it was on a temporary basis, at least we had become accustomed to the conditions, reached some semblance of normality and enjoyed the benefit of institutions that served our purposes. Above all, there had been a lofty goal in our minds that would reward our endurance – although when we were on the brink of reaching it, we had exchanged it for a new destination. We were removed from an atmosphere that primed us for going to Israel and placed in a situation where everyone was simply confused. The conditions were cramped, there was a lack of activity to divert the boredom of waiting, and many of the non-Jewish DPs were of Slavic origin. These people had escaped from their country because they had collaborated with the Germans, and they were anti-Semitic. This combination of factors frequently caused friction and at times the Italian police were called in to quell such confrontations.

Our decision was made, however, and we had to live with it. After about two months, we found ourselves on a train heading for Naples, where we boarded the Polish ship *Sobieski*. It was not exactly a pleasure cruiser and instead of a cabin we were accommodated in the hold, where there were countless rows of bunk beds. Except for sleeping, I spent all my time on deck. The irony was that we were sailing to the New World attended by a Polish crew and I remember the sounds of that language coming from the loudspeakers, accompanying me to the shore of Halifax. I am sure the announcements must have been in English as well but with the exception of a few words, English was still beyond my comprehension.

My first taste of America was, of course, Coca-Cola at ten cents a glass – a treat in which I indulged at least once a day.

Another dish in which I indulged generously was sweet little cucumbers (gherkins). Needless to say, this was my first sea voyage and at the beginning, the excitement that gripped me was equal to that during my first train ride to Brest Litovsk. No one had told me, however, that there was such a thing as seasickness. The first time the sea became a little rough, I discovered that I completely lacked sea legs and that I had eaten too many sweet little cucumbers (I do not touch those things anymore). We arrived in Halifax, where we disembarked into a huge hangar and were processed, and tags were attached to our garments, indicating our destination. I wandered around the huge building and discovered that when I passed a particular gate, I was handed a packet of cigarettes. I repeated this process five times and each time received another packet. 'Welcome to Canada. Have a packet of cigarettes.'

The train ride to Montreal was fascinating. The beauty of the countryside made a profound impression upon me, at least the parts that the billboards did not block off. A steward came over and showed us how to convert the seats we occupied into beds. *'Amerike Ganiv'*, we remarked. On 19 September 1948, we arrived in Montreal and were met by Mother's cousin. All our worldly possessions went into the trunk of the car, with plenty of room to spare, and not because the trunk was so spacious. It was the second time in my life that I had traveled in a car. Two landmarks made a particular impression on me as we drove to our new home. One was a gigantic billboard of a horse and the second was a cross on the mountain. Home was on St. Urbain Corner, Laurier, where we were boarders, sharing the premises with two brothers who occupied the two bedrooms and my family and I had the use of the living room.

By the end of the month, even before my parents were employed, I was undergoing tests, for the third time in my short life, to determine my scholastic standards. With the help of JOINT, who in the meantime paid for tuition, I was enrolled into the Talmud Torah, a parochial school. It seems that I presented something of a problem. I was able to converse in Hebrew, Yiddish, Ukrainian, Russian and Polish and even had a fair knowledge of Italian, but although I was familiar with the Latin alphabet, I could count my English vocabulary on the fingers of one hand, and as for French, it was Greek to me. I had traveled all over Europe and knew the geography of Israel in detail, but could not name the provinces of Canada. I had developed a political orientation and could discuss the differences between capitalism and socialism, but did not know that the king of England also 'ruled' over Canada. I could solve numerical problems in mathematics but could not read the questions.

I was no longer a DP. Finally my status had changed. Publicly I was known as a greenhorn and in the confines of the school, derisively, as a mocky. There was something physical about me that revealed my status: an aroma of the old country; sadness in the eyes; a discernable feeling of inferiority and discomfort. I was different but with an overwhelming desire to be like everyone else. It was a world with which, initially, I did not wish to have anything to do, but now I wanted to be a part of it. At the age of 13½ and in spite of being short for my age, I was at least a head taller than every other child in my class, because I started my education in grade three.

In my heart I was still committed to Israel but I wished to be like everyone else. In order to be like everyone else, I had to erase or suppress the terrible events of the Holocaust that molded my being. About forty-five years later I began to reveal – with an accuracy that still lingers in my mind – as a legacy to those who are dear to me, the details of why I had 'NO STRENGTH TO FORGET'.

The Library of Holocaust Testimonies

In the Shadow of Destruction
Recollections of Transnistria and Illegal Immigration to Eretz Israel, 1941–1947
Josef Govrin

Translated from the Hebrew original, *Be-Tzel ha-Avadon*, published by Beit Lohamei Haghetaot Press, 1999, in collaboration with Yad Vashem, Jerusalem, and the Center of Research of Romanian Jewry, the Hebrew University of Jerusalem.

This is a personal account of a young boy's struggle to survive the Holocaust in Transnistria. The descriptions are presented against the background of current events, combining personal recollections with an historic overview, before, during and after the Holocaust.

The author was 10 when Bessarabia and North Bucovina were invaded by the German and Romanian armies in July 1941. Interned with his mother in the Moghilev ghetto, the author describes the daily struggle to survive, and the economic and medical support received from the remaining Jewish communities in Romania. The ghetto was liberated by the Soviet Army in March 1944. In December 1946 the author and his mother embarked on a cargo ship on the Adriatic coast heading for Eretz Israel. After being detained by the British Navy and taken to Atlit, they were released in December 1947, on the eve of the Israel's War of Independence.

The book was chosen by a public committee of Israel's Ministry of Education as one of the 35 best books published in Israel in 1999.

March 2007, 116 pages
ISBN 978 0 85303 643 2
£16.50 / $25.00

The Library of Holocaust Testimonies

Sentenced to Life
The Story of a Survivor of the Lahwah Ghetto
Kopel Kolpanitzky
Translated from the Hebrew by Zvi Shulman

Kopel Kolpanitzky grew up in Lahwah, Byelorussia. His entire family was murdered in the Lahwah ghetto uprising against the Nazis, except for his father, who had previously been imprisoned by the Soviets. Living in the forests, he joined a partisan unit and then fought as a soldier in the Red Army. After the war he left the army and in trying to reach Eretz Yisrael almost reached the shores of Palestine before the ship he was on was stopped by the British and its passengers sent to a camp in Cyprus. A year later he finally arrived in Eretz Yisrael just before Israel's independence. He served in the Israel Defence Forces and later entered into business with his father, who had joined him in Israel in the early 1950s.

February 2007, 288 pages
ISBN 978 0 85303 695 1
£14.50 / $23.50

The Library of Holocaust Testimonies

The Girl in the Check Coat
Survival in Wartime Poland and a
New Life in Australia
Christine Winecki
Translated from the Hebrew by Chris Samplawski

Christine Winecki is a Holocaust child survivor. In her book she presents the story of her life, starting with the fond memories of her early childhood in south-eastern Poland, and then taking the reader through the turbulent years of the Second World War under Soviet and then German occupation. She depicts also the story of her future husband Oton – a survivor of a labour camp in Siberia – and their post-war life in Warsaw until the infamous events in 1968, which forced them to leave Poland and emigrate to Australia.

Apart from its biographical content the book is rich in observations on the historical, political and ethnographic aspects of the changing settings of the author's unfolding story. Her first book, *From Stanislawow to Australia* (in Polish), was published in 1999. Christine Winecki and her husband Oton live in Melbourne. They have two daughters and five grandchildren.

November 2006, 240 pages
ISBN 978 0 85303 657 7
£13.50 / $23.50

The Library of Holocaust Testimonies

In Hiding
Surviving an Abusive 'Protector' and the Nazi Occupation of Holland
Benno Benninga with William Halstead

When the German army invades the Netherlands in 1940, the Jewish family of Jacques and Reina Benninga, their teenage son Benno and daughter Mia attempt escape to England, but fail. They then try to comply with the Nazis' increasingly stringent anti-Jewish edicts until submission is intolerable and potentially life-threatening. Assuming the war would soon end, a Dutch couple agrees to hide the Benninga family for a large fee. As the Second World War and the Nazi occupation stretches on, their hostess becomes mentally and physically abusive. The couple's wartime business venture itself has the potential for disaster – she and her husband are active black marketeers, and a local police officer lives just across the road. Through it all, Jacques Benninga keeps a daily journal – a remarkable document which the authors have found an invaluable source to amplify Benno's gripping eyewitness memories of the family's nerve-wracking, life-threatening, two years in hiding.

November 2006, 188 pages
ISBN 978 0 85303 632 6
£13.50 / $23.50

The Library of Holocaust Testimonies

Till First Morning Light
Tales of Hungarian Jewry
Yaakov Barzilai
Translated from the Hebrew by Philip Simpson

Till First Morning Light is an autobiographical novel by a survivor of the Holocaust, the core of which is truth and the shell imagination. The story takes place in three countries – Hungary, Austria and Germany – during the years of Nazi rule.

The story depicts a cross-section of Hungarian Jewry, whose bitter fate ended one year after the battle of Stalingrad and three months before the invasion of Normandy by the Allied forces.

Lyrically told, the story moves forwards and backwards – associative and not chronological, the past and the present mixed together. The book expresses the meeting between Holocaust and humour. The characters are honest and innocent people, happy and angry, who quarrel and conciliate, love and marry, laugh and joke, up until the final moments of their lives. They are people plucked from their homes, from their work, from their children and their schools, the flames of their lives extinguished before their time. Between all the characters and the plot there is a principal character, the mother of the narrator. With her courage, her desire to live and her love for family she succeeds in bringing her children to the shores of safety, even if the father of the family remains behind in the death camp Bergen-Belsen. Time after time she confronts the angel of death. She prevails throughout all these confrontations and the angel of death withdraws.

The book was written with two hands – one hand strikes and the other strokes. During the same period, all the trains travelled in one direction. The author's train travelled in two directions in order to tell the events of the most horrific period in human history to future generations: to go through the darkness until the first morning light.

September 2007, 148 pages
ISBN 978 0 85303 631 9
£14.50 / $23.50

The Library of Holocaust Testimonies

My Hometown Concentration Camp
A Survivor's Account of Life in the Kraków Ghetto and Plaszów Concentration Camp
Bernard Offen, with Norman Jacobs

My Hometown Concentration Camp tells the story of the young Bernard Offen's endurance and survival of the Kraków Ghetto and five concentration camps, including Plaszów and Auschwitz-Birkenau, until his liberation near Dachau by American troops in 1945.

The author tells of his experiences in the ghetto and camps and how he set out, after the war, in search of his brothers, eventually finding them in Italy with the Polish Army. Having returned to the United States, Bernard Offen was drafted into the US Army to serve in the Korean War. After the war he founded his own business and built a family, both helping to restore a sense of normality to his life. This was the start of his own unique process of healing that led, ultimately, to his retirement and decision to dedicate his life to educating audiences around the world about his experiences during the Holocaust.

The testimony of one man, Bernard Offen's story recounts his one-man journey across America, Europe, Israel and back to his native Poland, and his development as a filmmaker, educator and healer.

My Hometown Concentration Camp will touch readers through the strength of the author's self-determination to attempt to confront and conquer the traumatic experiences he witnessed as a young man.

September 2007, 176 pages
ISBN 978 0 85303 636 4
£14.50 / $23.50